THE WHO'S BUYING SERIES
BY THE NEW STRATEGIST EDITORS

Who's Buying at Restaurants and Carry-Outs

10th EDITION

New Strategist Press
26 Austin Avenue
P.O. Box 635
Amityville, NY 11701
Toll-free: 800 848-0842; Phone: 631 608-8795
Fax: 631 691-1770
www.newstrategist.com

ISBN 978-1-935775-94-2

Printed in the United States of America

Contents

Household Spending at Restaurants and Carry-Outs by Product Category, 2010

About the Data in *Who's Buying at Restaurants and Carry-Outs*

Introduction

The spending data in *Who's Buying at Restaurants and Carry-Outs* are based on the Bureau of Labor Statistics' Consumer Expenditure Survey, an ongoing, nationwide survey of household spending. The Consumer Expenditure Survey is a complete accounting of household expenditures. It includes everything from big-ticket items, such as homes and cars, to small purchases like laundry detergent and videos. The survey does not include expenditures by government, business, or institutions. The data in this report are from the 2010 Consumer Expenditure Survey, unless otherwise noted.

To produce this report, New Strategist Publications analyzed the Consumer Expenditure Survey's average household spending data in a variety of ways, calculating household spending indexes, aggregate (or total) household spending, and market shares. This report shows spending data by age, household income, household type, race, Hispanic origin, region of residence, and education. These analyses are presented in two formats—for all product categories by demographic characteristic and for all demographic characteristics by product category.

Definition of Consumer Unit

The Consumer Expenditure Survey uses the consumer unit rather than the household as the sampling unit. The term "household" is used interchangeably with the term "consumer unit" in this report for convenience, although they are not exactly the same. Some households contain more than one consumer unit.

The Bureau of Labor Statistics defines consumer units as either: (1) members of a household who are related by blood, marriage, adoption, or other legal arrangements; (2) a person living alone or sharing a household with others or living as a roomer in a private home or lodging house or in permanent living quarters in a hotel or motel, but who is financially independent; or (3) two or more persons living together who pool their income to make joint expenditure decisions. The bureau defines financial independence in terms of "the three major expense categories: housing, food, and other living expenses. To be considered financially independent, at least two of the three major expense categories have to be provided by the respondent."

The Census Bureau uses the household as its sampling unit in the decennial census and in the monthly Current Population Survey. The Census Bureau's household "consists of all persons who occupy a housing unit. A house, an apartment or other groups of rooms, or a single room is regarded as a housing unit when it is occupied or intended for occupancy as separate living quarters; that is, when the occupants do not live and eat with any other persons in the structure and there is direct access from the outside or through a common hall."

The definition goes on to specify that "a household includes the related family members and all the unrelated persons, if any, such as lodgers, foster children, wards, or employees who share the housing unit. A person living alone in a housing unit or a group of unrelated persons sharing a housing unit as partners is also counted as a household. The count of households excludes group quarters."

Because there can be more than one consumer unit in a household, consumer units outnumber households by several million. Young adults under age 25 head most of the additional consumer units.

How to Use the Tables in This Report

The starting point for all calculations are the unpublished, detailed average household spending data collected by the Consumer Expenditure Survey. These numbers are shown on the report's average spending tables and on each of the product-specific tables. New Strategist's editors calculated the other figures in the report based on the average figures. The indexed spending tables and the indexed spending column (Best Customers) on the product-specific tables reveal whether spending by households in a given segment is above or below the average for all households and by how much. The total (or aggregate) spending tables show the overall size of the market. The market share tables and market share column (Biggest Customers) on the product-specific tables reveal how much spending each household segment controls. These analyses are described in detail below.

• **Average Spending.** The average spending figures show the average annual spending of households at restaurants and carry-out establishments in 2010. The Consumer Expenditure Survey produces average spending data for all households in a segment, e.g., all households with a householder aged 25 to 34, not just for those who purchased the item. When examining spending data, it is important to remember that by including both purchasers and nonpurchasers in the calculation, the average is less than the amount spent on the item by buyers. (See Table 1 for the percentage of households that spent at restaurants and carry-out establishments in 2010 and how much the purchasers spent.)

Because average spending figures include both buyers and nonbuyers, they reveal spending patterns by demographic characteristic. By knowing who is most likely to spend on an item, marketers can target their advertising and promotions more efficiently, and businesses can determine the market potential of a product or service in a city or neighborhood. By multiplying the average amount households spend on full-service dinners by the number of households in an area, for example, a restaurant owner can estimate the potential size of the local sit-down dining market.

• **Indexed Spending (Best Customers).** The indexed spending figures compare the spending of each household segment with that of the average household. To compute the indexes, New Strategist divides the average amount each household segment spends on an item by average household spending and multiplies the resulting figure by 100.

An index of 100 is the average for all households. An index of 125 means the spending of a household segment is 25 percent above average (100 plus 25). An index of 75 indicates spending that is 25 percent below the average for all households (100 minus 25). Indexed spending figures identify the best customers for a product or service. Households with an index of 178 for fast-food lunches, for example, are a strong market for this product. Those with an index below 100 are either a weak or an underserved market.

Spending indexes can reveal hidden markets—household segments with a high propensity to buy a particular product or service but which are overshadowed by household segments that account for a larger share of the market. Householders aged 65 to 74, for example, account for 13 percent of the market for full-service breakfasts, less than the 16 percent share accounted for by householders aged 25 to 34. But a look at the indexed spending figures reveals that, in fact, the older householders are the better customers. Householders aged 65 to 74 spend 18 percent more than the average household on full-service breakfasts, while householders aged 25 to 34 spend 6 percent less than the average household on this item. The owners of restaurants can use this information to target their best customers.

Note that because of sampling errors, small differences in index values may be insignificant. But the broader patterns revealed by indexes can guide marketers to the best customers.

• **Total (Aggregate) Spending.** To produce the total (aggregate) spending figures, New Strategist multiplies average spending by the number of households in a segment. The result is the dollar size of the total household market and of each market segment. All totals are shown in thousands of dollars. To convert the numbers in the total spending tables to dollars, you must append "000" to the number. For example, households headed by people aged 45 to 54 spent nearly $18 billion ($17,882,794,000) on full-service dinners in 2010.

When comparing the total spending figures in this report with total spending estimates from the Bureau of Economic Analysis, other government agencies, or trade associations, keep in mind that the Consumer Expenditure Survey includes only household spending, not spending by businesses or institutions. Sales data also differ from household spending totals because sales figures for consumer products include the value of goods sold to industries, government, and foreign markets, which may be a significant proportion of sales.

• **Market Shares (Biggest Customers).** New Strategist produces market share figures by converting total (aggregate) spending data into percentages. To calculate the percentage of total spending on an item that is controlled by each demographic segment—i.e., its market share—each segment's total spending on an item is divided by aggregate household spending on the item.

Market shares reveal the biggest customers—the demographic segments that account for the largest share of spending on a particular product or service. In 2010, for example, married couples with children at home accounted for 36 percent of spending on fast-food dinners, a much greater share than their 23 percent of consumer units. By targeting only these consumers, fast-food restaurants can reach a large proportion of their customers. There is a danger here, however. By single-mindedly targeting the biggest customers, businesses cannot nurture potential growth markets. With competition for customers more heated than ever, targeting potential markets is increasingly important to business survival.

• **Product-Specific Tables.** The product-specific tables reveal at a glance the demographic characteristics of spending by individual product category. These tables show average spending, indexed spending (Best Customers), and market shares (Biggest Customers) by age, income, household type, race and Hispanic origin, region of residence, and education. If you want to see the spending pattern for an individual product at a glance, these are the tables for you.

History and Methodology of the Consumer Expenditure Survey

The Consumer Expenditure Survey is an ongoing study of the day-to-day spending of American households. In taking the survey, government interviewers collect spending data on products and services as well as the amount and sources of household income, changes in saving and debt, and demographic and economic characteristics of household members. The Bureau of the Census collects data for the Consumer Expenditure Survey under contract with the Bureau of Labor Statistics, which is responsible for analysis and release of the survey data.

Since the late 19th century, the federal government has conducted expenditure surveys about every 10 years. Although the results have been used for a variety of purposes, their primary application is to track consumer prices. In 1980, the Consumer Expenditure Survey became continuous with annual release of data. The survey is used to update prices for the market basket of products and services used in calculating the Consumer Price Index.

The Consumer Expenditure Survey consists of two separate surveys: an interview survey and a diary survey. In the interview portion of the survey, respondents are asked each quarter for five consecutive quarters to report their expenditures for the previous three months. The interview survey records purchases of big-ticket items such as houses, cars, and major appliances, and recurring expenses such as insurance premiums, utility payments, and rent. The interview component covers about 95 percent of all expenditures.

The diary survey records expenditures on small, frequently purchased items during a two-week period. These detailed records include expenses for food and beverages purchased in grocery stores and at restaurants, as well as other items such as tobacco, housekeeping supplies, nonprescription drugs, and personal care products and services. The diary survey is intended to capture expenditures respondents are likely to forget or recall incorrectly over longer periods of time.

Two separate, nationally representative samples are used for the interview and diary surveys. For the interview survey, about 7,000 consumer units are interviewed on a rotating panel basis each quarter for five consecutive quarters. Another 7,000 consumer units kept weekly diaries of spending for two consecutive weeks. Data collection is carried out in 91 areas of the country.

The Bureau of Labor Statistics reviews, audits, and cleanses the data, then weights them to reflect the number and characteristics of all U.S. consumer units. Like any sample survey, the Consumer Expenditure Survey is subject to two major types of error. Nonsampling error occurs when respondents misinterpret questions or interviewers are inconsistent in the way they ask questions or record answers. Respondents may forget items, recall expenses incorrectly, or deliberately give wrong answers. A respondent may remember how much he or she spent at the grocery store but forget the items picked up at a local convenience store. Mistakes during the various stages of data processing and refinement can also cause nonsampling error.

Sampling error occurs when a sample does not accurately represent the population it is supposed to represent. This kind of error is present in every sample-based survey and is minimized by using a proper sampling procedure. Standard error tables documenting the extent of sampling error in the Consumer Expenditure Survey are available from the Bureau of Labor Statistics at http://www.bls.gov/cex/csxstnderror.htm.

Although the Consumer Expenditure Survey is the best source of information about the spending behavior of American households, it should be treated with caution because of the above problems.

For More Information

To find out more about the Consumer Expenditure Survey, contact the specialists at the Bureau of Labor Statistics at (202) 691-6900, or visit the Consumer Expenditure Survey home page at http://www.bls.gov/cex/. The web site includes news releases, technical documentation, and current and historical summary-level data. The detailed average spending data shown in this report are available from the Bureau of Labor Statistics only by special request.

For a comprehensive look at detailed household spending data for all products and services, see the 17th edition of *Household Spending: Who Spends How Much on What*. New Strategist's books are available in hardcopy or as downloads with links to the Excel version of each table. Find out more by visiting http://www.newstrategist.com or by calling 1-800-848-0842.

Table 1. Percent reporting expenditure and amount spent, average week, 2010

(percent of consumer units reporting expenditure and amount spent by purchasers during the average week, 2010)

	average week	
	percent reporting expenditure	amount spent by purchasers
RESTAURANTS AND CARRY-OUTS	**69.5%**	**$57.61**
Lunch	**51.0**	**27.41**
At fast-food restaurants*	39.1	17.28
At full-service restaurants	19.7	27.85
At vending machines, mobile vendors	3.1	4.81
At employer and school cafeterias	9.6	16.48
Dinner	**45.1**	**42.13**
At fast-food restaurants*	29.7	21.43
At full-service restaurants	25.1	49.54
At vending machines, mobile vendors	0.7	7.46
At employer and school cafeterias	1.0	13.46
Snacks and nonalcoholic beverages	**31.0**	**9.66**
At fast-food restaurants*	22.8	8.65
At full-service restaurants	5.9	9.31
At vending machines, mobile vendors	9.1	3.96
At employer and school cafeterias	2.7	4.09
Breakfast and brunch	**28.4**	**14.36**
At fast-food restaurants*	21.8	9.75
At full-service restaurants	8.9	18.34
At vending machines, mobile vendors	1.6	3.87
At employer and school cafeterias	2.8	9.45

* The category fast-food restaurants also includes take-out, delivery, concession stands, buffets, and cafeterias other than employer and school.
Source: Calculations by New Strategist based on the 2010 Consumer Expenditure Survey

Household Spending Trends, 2000 to 2010

As American households struggle with the aftermath of the Great Recession, their spending has declined. Average household spending climbed 9 percent between 2000 and 2006, peaking at $52,349 (in 2010 dollars). Then the recession set in. Average household spending fell 8 percent between 2006 and 2010, to $48,109.

On many products and services, households boosted their spending between 2000 and 2006 and cut back between 2006 and 2010. Average household spending on alcoholic beverages, for example, grew by a substantial 14 percent between 2000 and 2006, after adjusting for inflation. Between 2006 and 2010, household spending on alcoholic beverages fell 23 percent. Similarly, average household spending on food away from home (primarily restaurant meals) increased 8 percent between 2000 and 2006, then fell 14 percent between 2006 and 2010. Spending on mortgage interest increased by 21 percent between 2000 and 2006 as the housing bubble inflated, then fell 17 percent between 2006 and 2010 as the bubble burst and foreclosures became common.

Despite the recession, the cost of living continued to rise. Consequently, the average household was forced to spend more on necessities such as health care. Average household spending on health care climbed 14 percent between 2000 and 2006 and by another 6 percent between 2006 and 2010. Behind the continuing increase was the rise in health insurance premiums, average household spending on health insurance growing by 27 percent between 2000 and 2006 and by another 16 percent between 2006 and 2010. The average household spent 13 percent less on drugs in 2010 than in 2006 as the Medicare prescription drug program kicked in and lowered drug costs for older Americans.

Spending on nondiscretionary items fits the downward trend with one exception. The average household spent 36 percent more on the category "pets, toys, and playground equipment" in 2010 than in 2006, after adjusting for inflation. Most of the increase was accounted for by much greater spending on pet medicines such as heartworm and flea treatments. Spending on entertainment, which had seen increases until 2009, declined 9 percent between that year and 2010 and now also fits the overall pattern with a 3 percent decline for the 2006-to-2010 period despite higher cable bills, the popularity of big-screen television sets, and much more spending on pets.

Some spending categories experienced a decline in both time periods. Despite the rising homeownership rate, spending on household furnishings and equipment fell 6 percent between 2000 and 2006 and another 21 percent between 2006 and 2010. Households were devoting so much to mortgage payments that they were forced to reduce spending on items for outfitting their home. Spending on apparel continued its long-term downward trend in both time periods as well.

Spending on food at home fell 3 percent in the 2000-to-2006 time period, then declined another 2 percent from 2006 to 2010 although Americans ate more often at home as evidenced by the 14 percent decline in spending on restaurant meals between 2006 and 2010. These spending shifts, and the sharp reduction in spending on so many items, show that American consumers have become not just cautious spenders but penny-pinchers—with enormous consequences for our economy.

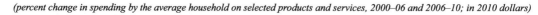

Households spent more, then cut back, on many items

(percent change in spending by the average household on selected products and services, 2000–06 and 2006–10; in 2010 dollars)

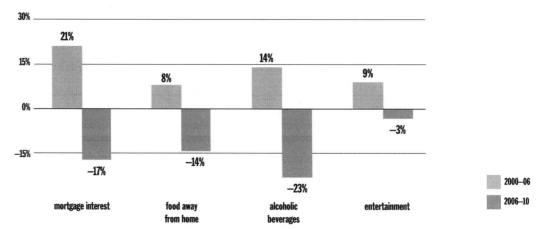

Table 2. Household spending trends, 2000 to 2010

(average annual spending of total consumer units, 2000, 2006, 2009, and 2010; percent change, 2006–10, 2000–06, and 2000–10; in 2010 dollars)

	2010	2009	2006	2000	percent change 2006–10	2000–06	2000–10
Number of consumer units (in 000s)	121,107	120,847	118,843	109,367	1.9%	8.7%	10.7%
Average before-tax income of consumer units	$62,481	$63,888	$65,474	$56,539	–4.6	15.8	10.5
Average annual spending of consumer units	**48,109**	**49,872**	**52,349**	**48,176**	**–8.1**	**8.7**	**–0.1**
FOOD	**6,129**	**6,477**	**6,610**	**6,532**	**–7.3**	**1.2**	**–6.2**
Food at home	**3,624**	**3,815**	**3,696**	**3,825**	**–1.9**	**–3.4**	**–5.3**
Cereals and bakery products	502	514	482	574	4.1	–15.9	–12.5
Cereals and cereal products	165	176	155	198	6.7	–21.7	–16.5
Bakery products	337	339	329	376	2.5	–12.6	–10.4
Meats, poultry, fish, and eggs	784	855	862	1,007	–9.1	–14.4	–22.1
Beef	217	230	255	301	–15.0	–15.3	–28.0
Pork	149	171	170	211	–12.3	–19.7	–29.5
Other meats	117	116	114	128	3.0	–11.2	–8.5
Poultry	138	157	153	184	–9.5	–16.9	–24.8
Fish and seafood	117	137	132	139	–11.3	–5.3	–16.0
Eggs	46	45	40	43	14.9	–7.0	6.8
Dairy products	380	413	398	412	–4.5	–3.3	–7.7
Fresh milk and cream	141	146	151	166	–6.9	–8.7	–15.0
Other dairy products	240	266	247	244	–2.7	0.9	–1.8
Fruits and vegeTable s	679	667	640	660	6.0	–2.9	2.9
Fresh fruits	232	224	211	206	10.0	2.2	12.4
Fresh vegeTable s	210	212	209	201	0.6	3.7	4.3
Processed fruits	113	120	118	146	–4.2	–19.0	–22.4
Processed vegeTable s	124	112	103	106	20.7	–3.4	16.6
Other food at home	1,278	1,365	1,311	1,174	–2.5	11.7	8.9
Sugar and other sweets	132	143	135	148	–2.4	–8.7	–10.9
Fats and oils	103	104	93	105	10.7	–11.5	–2.0
Miscellaneous foods	667	727	678	553	–1.6	22.6	20.5
Nonalcoholic beverages	333	343	359	317	–7.3	13.4	5.2
Food prepared by consumer unit on trips	43	50	47	51	–7.5	–8.2	–15.1
Food away from home	**2,505**	**2,662**	**2,914**	**2,706**	**–14.0**	**7.7**	**–7.4**
ALCOHOLIC BEVERAGES	**412**	**442**	**538**	**471**	**–23.4**	**14.1**	**–12.5**
HOUSING	**16,557**	**17,172**	**17,702**	**15,599**	**–6.5**	**13.5**	**6.1**
Shelter	**9,812**	**10,240**	**10,463**	**9,008**	**–6.2**	**16.1**	**8.9**
Owned dwellings	6,277	6,650	7,048	5,827	–10.9	20.9	7.7
Mortgage interest and charges	3,351	3,653	4,059	3,342	–17.4	21.5	0.3
Property taxes	1,814	1,841	1,784	1,442	1.7	23.7	25.8
Maintenance, repair, insurance, other expenses	1,112	1,157	1,206	1,045	–7.8	15.4	6.4
Rented dwellings	2,900	2,907	2,801	2,576	3.5	8.8	12.6
Other lodging	635	683	613	605	3.5	1.3	4.9
Utilities, fuels, and public services	**3,660**	**3,705**	**3,674**	**3,152**	**–0.4**	**16.6**	**16.1**
Natural gas	440	491	551	389	–20.1	41.6	13.2
Electricity	1,413	1,400	1,369	1,154	3.2	18.7	22.5
Fuel oil and other fuels	140	143	149	123	–6.2	21.5	14.0
Telephone services	1,178	1,181	1,176	1,111	0.2	5.9	6.1
Water and other public services	489	489	429	375	13.9	14.6	30.5
Household services	**1,007**	**1,028**	**1,025**	**866**	**–1.8**	**18.4**	**16.3**
Personal services	340	395	425	413	–20.0	3.0	–17.6
Other household services	667	632	600	453	11.1	32.4	47.1
Housekeeping supplies	**612**	**670**	**692**	**610**	**–11.6**	**13.4**	**0.3**
Laundry and cleaning supplies	150	159	163	166	–8.2	–1.5	–9.6
Other household products	329	366	357	286	–7.8	24.7	15.0
Postage and stationery	132	145	172	160	–23.2	7.8	–17.3

	2010	2009	2006	2000	percent change 2006–10	percent change 2000–06	percent change 2000–10
Household furnishings and equipment	$1,467	$1,531	$1,847	$1,961	−20.6%	−5.8%	−25.2%
Household textiles	102	126	167	134	−38.8	24.1	−24.0
Furniture	355	349	501	495	−29.1	1.1	−28.3
Floor coverings	36	30	52	56	−30.7	−6.8	−35.4
Major appliances	209	197	261	239	−19.8	8.9	−12.7
Small appliances and miscellaneous housewares	107	95	118	110	−9.2	7.0	−2.9
Miscellaneous household equipment	657	733	750	926	−12.3	−19.0	−29.0
APPAREL AND RELATED SERVICES	1,700	1,753	2,027	2,350	−16.1	−13.8	−27.7
Men and boys	382	389	480	557	−20.5	−13.8	−31.4
Men, aged 16 or older	304	309	382	436	−20.4	−12.3	−30.2
Boys, aged 2 to 15	78	80	98	122	−20.8	−19.0	−35.8
Women and girls	663	689	812	918	−18.4	−11.5	−27.8
Women, aged 16 or older	562	570	680	769	−17.4	−11.5	−26.9
Girls, aged 2 to 15	101	120	132	149	−23.5	−11.7	−32.4
Children under age 2	91	92	104	104	−12.4	0.0	−12.4
Footwear	303	328	329	434	−7.9	−24.3	−30.2
Other apparel products and services	261	253	303	337	−13.8	−10.1	−22.5
TRANSPORTATION	7,677	7,784	9,202	9,392	−16.6	−2.0	−18.3
Vehicle purchases	2,588	2,701	3,700	4,328	−30.1	−14.5	−40.2
Cars and trucks, new	1,219	1,318	1,945	2,032	−37.3	−4.3	−40.0
Cars and trucks, used	1,318	1,325	1,696	2,241	−22.3	−24.3	−41.2
Gasoline and motor oil	2,132	2,019	2,409	1,635	−11.5	47.3	30.4
Other vehicle expenses	2,464	2,578	2,547	2,888	−3.3	−11.8	−14.7
Vehicle finance charges	243	286	322	415	−24.6	−22.4	−41.5
Maintenance and repairs	787	745	744	790	5.8	−5.8	−0.4
Vehicle insurance	1,010	1,093	958	985	5.4	−2.7	2.5
Vehicle rentals, leases, licenses, other charges	423	454	521	698	−18.9	−25.3	−39.4
Public transportation	493	487	546	541	−9.7	1.0	−8.8
HEALTH CARE	3,157	3,177	2,992	2,616	5.5	14.4	20.7
Health insurance	1,831	1,814	1,585	1,245	15.6	27.3	47.1
Medical services	722	748	725	719	−0.4	0.8	0.4
Drugs	485	494	556	527	−12.8	5.5	−7.9
Medical supplies	119	121	127	125	−6.0	0.9	−5.1
ENTERTAINMENT	2,504	2,737	2,570	2,359	−2.6	8.9	6.1
Fees and admissions	581	638	655	652	−11.4	0.5	−10.9
Audio and visual equipment and services	954	991	980	788	−2.6	24.4	21.1
Pets, toys, and playground equipment	606	701	446	423	36.0	5.4	43.3
Other entertainment products and services	364	407	488	498	−25.4	−2.0	−26.9
PERSONAL CARE PRODUCTS AND SERVICES	582	606	633	714	−8.0	−11.4	−18.5
READING	100	112	127	185	−21.0	−31.5	−45.9
EDUCATION	1,074	1,086	960	800	11.8	20.0	34.2
TOBACCO PRODUCTS AND SMOKING SUPPLIES	362	386	354	404	2.3	−12.4	−10.4
MISCELLANEOUS	849	829	915	983	−7.2	−6.9	−13.6
CASH CONTRIBUTIONS	1,633	1,751	2,022	1,509	−19.2	33.9	8.2
PERSONAL INSURANCE AND PENSIONS	5,373	5,561	5,700	4,261	−5.7	33.8	26.1
Life and other personal insurance	318	314	348	505	−8.7	−31.1	−37.1
Pensions and Social Security*	5,054	5,247	5,352	3,756	−5.6	–	–
PERSONAL TAXES	1,769	2,139	2,631	3,947	−32.8	−33.4	−55.2
Federal income taxes	1,136	1,427	1,851	3,051	−38.6	−39.3	−62.8
State and local income taxes	482	533	561	712	−14.1	−21.1	−32.3
Other taxes	151	180	218	185	−30.9	18.2	−18.3
GIFTS FOR PEOPLE IN OTHER HOUSEHOLDS	1,029	1,085	1,248	1,371	−17.6	−9.0	−25.0

*Recent spending on pensions and Social Security is not comparable with 2000 because of changes in methodology.

Note: Spending by category does not add to total spending because gift spending is also included in the preceding product and service categories and personal taxes are not included in the total. "–" means data are not comparable.

Source: Bureau of Labor Statistics, 2000, 2006, 2009, and 2010 Consumer Expenditure Surveys, Internet site http://www.bls.gov/cex/; calculations by New Strategist

Household Spending at Restaurants and Carry-Outs, 2006 to 2010

Between 2006 and 2010, average household spending at restaurants and carry-outs fell by 15 percent, after adjusting for inflation, as households cut their spending in the depressed economy. Despite the decline, households still spend a considerable portion of their food dollar at restaurants. What once was a special occasion—eating out—has become a necessity over the past few decades as busy two-earner families try to save time. The Bureau of Labor Statistics reports that during the average week of 2010, 69 percent of households purchased food from restaurants and spent an average of $58.

The average household spent $2,304 at restaurants in 2010, 64 percent of what it spent on groceries ($3,624). Among some demographic segments, the proportion of the food dollar devoted to restaurants is even higher. Householders aged 25 to 34 spend 76 percent as much eating out as on groceries, the figure falling with age to 46 percent among householders aged 75 or older. Among households with incomes of $100,000 or more, the figure is 80 percent. People who live alone also spend 80 percent as much eating out as on groceries.

Households devote more of their restaurant dollars to dinners (43 percent) than to lunches (32 percent). Restaurant meals on trips (which the survey does not break down by type of restaurant) account for 10 percent of restaurant spending, breakfasts for 9 percent, and snacks for 7 percent.

The average household devotes less of the eating-out dollar to fast food than to full-service restaurants. Of the $2,304 the average household spent on eating out in 2010, fast-food restaurants captured a 39 percent share, while full-service restaurants took a larger 45 percent. The remainder is spent at employer and school cafeterias, vending machines, mobile vendors, and on trips.

Older Americans, particularly empty-nesters, are far more likely to choose full-service over fast-food restaurants. Among householders under age 25, fast food claims 47 percent of the restaurant dollar. The fast-food share declines with age to just 25 percent of restaurant spending among householders aged 75 or older. The demands of children explain changing restaurant preferences with age. Among household types, single parents devote the largest share of their dining-out dollars to fast-food restaurants (51 percent), followed by households with preschoolers (44 percent). In contrast, married couples without children at home (most of them empty-nesters) spend only 30 percent of their restaurant dollars in fast-food establishments.

Table 3. Restaurant and carry-out spending, 2006 and 2010

(average annual and percent distribution of household spending at restaurants and carry-outs by category, 2006 and 2010; percent and percentage point change in spending, 2006–10, in 2010 dollars; ranked by amount spent)

	2010 average household spending	2006 average household spending (in 2010$)	percent change 2006–10
AVERAGE ANNUAL SPENDING			
AVERAGE HOUSEHOLD SPENDING AT RESTAURANTS BY TYPE OF MEAL			
Total restaurant spending	**$2,304.03**	**$2,695.75**	**−14.5%**
Dinner	986.99	1,160.26	−14.9
Lunch	726.61	831.36	−12.6
Restaurant meals on trips	223.08	262.76	−15.1
Breakfast and brunch	212.05	252.48	−16.0
Snacks and nonalcoholic beverages	155.29	188.88	−17.8
AVERAGE HOUSEHOLD SPENDING BY TYPE OF MEAL AND RESTAURANT			
Total restaurant spending	**$2,304.03**	**$2,695.75**	**−14.5%**
Dinner	986.99	1,160.26	−14.9
At full-service restaurants	645.44	783.71	−17.6
At fast-food restaurants*	331.42	365.48	−9.3
Lunch	726.61	831.36	−12.6
At fast-food restaurants*	351.38	400.27	−12.2
At full-service restaurants	285.15	325.67	−12.4
At employer and school cafeterias	82.14	93.18	−11.9
Restaurant meals on trips	223.08	262.76	−15.1
Breakfast and brunch	212.05	252.48	−16.0
At fast-food restaurants*	110.61	117.02	−5.5
At full-service restaurants	84.81	118.95	−28.7
Snacks and nonalcoholic beverages	155.29	188.88	−17.8
At fast-food restaurants*	102.25	116.22	−12.0
At full-service restaurants	28.53	32.23	−11.5
At vending machines, mobile vendors	18.59	33.05	−43.8
At employer and school cafeterias	5.93	7.38	−19.6

	2010	2006	percentage point change 2006–10
PERCENT DISTRIBUTION OF SPENDING			
AVERAGE HOUSEHOLD SPENDING AT RESTAURANTS BY TYPE OF MEAL			
Total restaurant spending	**100.0%**	**100.0%**	–
Dinner	42.8	43.0	–0.2
Lunch	31.5	30.8	0.7
Restaurant meals on trips	9.7	9.7	–0.1
Breakfast and brunch	9.2	9.4	–0.2
Snacks and nonalcoholic beverages	6.7	7.0	–0.3

	2010	2006	percentage point change 2006–10
AVERAGE HOUSEHOLD SPENDING BY TYPE OF MEAL AND RESTAURANT			
Total restaurant spending	**100.0%**	**100.0%**	–
Dinner	42.8	43.0	–0.2
At full-service restaurants	28.0	29.1	–1.1
At fast-food restaurants*	14.4	13.6	0.8
Lunch	31.5	30.8	0.7
At fast-food restaurants*	15.3	14.8	0.4
At full-service restaurants	12.4	12.1	0.3
At employer and school cafeterias	3.6	3.5	0.1
Restaurant meals on trips	9.7	9.7	–0.1
Breakfast and brunch	9.2	9.4	–0.2
At fast-food restaurants*	4.8	4.3	0.5
At full-service restaurants	3.7	4.4	–0.7
Snacks and nonalcoholic beverages	6.7	7.0	–0.3
At fast-food restaurants*	4.4	4.3	0.1
At full-service restaurants	1.2	1.2	0.0
At vending machines, mobile vendors	0.8	1.2	–0.4
At employer and school cafeterias	0.3	0.3	0.0

* The category fast-food restaurants also includes take-out, delivery, concession stands, buffets, and cafeterias other than employer and school.
Note: Subcategories do not add to total because not all types of restaurants or meals are shown. "–" means not applicable.
Source: Bureau of Labor Statistics, 2006 and 2010 Consumer Expenditure Surveys; calculations by New Strategist

Household Spending at Restaurants and Carry-Outs by Demographic Characteristic, 2010

Spending by Age

Not surprisingly, the middle aged spend the most at restaurants and carry-outs because they have the highest incomes and the largest households. Householders aged 35 to 44 spend 29 percent more than the average household at restaurants and carry-outs. But householders under age 25 spend by far the most on dinner at employer and school cafeterias, while householders aged 65 to 74 spend more than the other age groups on full-service breakfasts. Householders ranging in age from 45 to 74 spend the most on restaurant and carry-out food on trips.

Spending by Household Income

The most-affluent households spend much more than average at restaurants and carry-outs. In 2010, households with incomes of $100,000 or more spent twice the average at restaurants and carry-outs. The $100,000-or-more income group accounts for 35 percent of household spending on eating out—more than double their 17 percent share of households. These affluent households control 41 percent of spending on full-service restaurant dinners and 47 percent of spending on restaurant food while traveling.

Spending by Household Type

Married couples with school-aged children spend more eating out than any other household type—49 percent more than average in 2010. Married couples with adult children at home spend more on lunch at fast-food restaurants than other household types because they have more workers. Married couples without children at home spend more than other household types on full-service breakfasts and lunches as well as on restaurant food while traveling. Single parents spend over three times the average on breakfasts at employer and school cafeterias and over twice the average on cafeteria lunches.

Spending by Race and Hispanic Origin

Asian households spend 42 percent more than the average household on restaurant meals—more than any other racial or ethnic group. Hispanic households spend just about an average amount on this category, while black households spend 30 percent less. Asians spend above average on most restaurant categories and outspend the other racial groups and Hispanics on a great number. Black householders spend more than average on only three categories: breakfasts at employer and school cafeterias, fast-food dinners, and fast-food breakfasts. Hispanics spend more than the other groups on breakfasts, lunches, and dinners at vending machines and mobile vendors.

Spending by Region

Average annual household spending on restaurant and carry-out food is highest in the West ($2,647) and Northeast ($2,604) and lowest in the Midwest ($1,969). Households in the Northeast are the biggest spenders on fast-food breakfasts (29 percent above average), but they spend 3 percent less than average on fast-food lunches. Households in the West spend more than those in other regions on lunches overall as well as on full-service breakfasts. Households in the Midwest are the biggest spenders on lunches and dinners from vending machines and mobile vendors as well as cafeteria breakfasts. The typical Southern household spends notably more than the national average on only one category: full-service lunches.

Spending by Education

Spending on eating out rises with education, in part because educated householders have higher incomes. College graduates spend 43 percent more than the average household at restaurants and carry-outs, including spending 54 and 63 percent above average on full-service lunches and dinners, respectively. The 30 percent of consumer units that are headed by college graduates control 46 percent of spending on full-service lunches, 48 percent of spending on full service dinners, and 55 percent of spending on restaurant meals while traveling.

Table 4. Restaurants and Carry-Outs: Average spending by age, 2010

(average annual spending of consumer units on restaurant and carry-out food, by age of consumer unit reference person, 2010)

	total consumer units	under 25	25 to 34	35 to 44	45 to 54	55 to 64	65 to 74	75+
Number of consumer units (in 000s)	121,107	8,034	20,166	21,912	25,054	21,359	13,031	11,551
Number of persons per consumer unit	2.5	2.0	2.9	3.3	2.8	2.2	1.9	1.6
Average before-tax income of consumer units	$62,481.00	$26,881.00	$59,613.00	$76,128.00	$79,589.00	$68,906.00	$49,711.00	$31,782.00
Average spending of consumer units, total	48,108.84	27,482.77	46,617.48	55,945.67	57,788.25	50,899.73	41,433.85	31,528.55
RESTAURANTS AND CARRY-OUTS	2,304.02	1,732.00	2,529.90	2,974.07	2,549.40	2,184.99	1,877.43	1,212.27
Lunch	726.61	582.11	798.23	955.44	773.11	665.18	583.13	446.83
At fast-food restaurants*	351.38	309.91	445.15	470.00	379.18	324.47	219.81	130.90
At full-service restaurants	285.15	175.25	270.00	310.45	266.53	294.55	341.40	301.38
At vending machines, mobile vendors	7.94	10.47	9.80	9.55	9.28	8.04	2.08	3.39
At employer and school cafeterias	82.14	86.47	73.29	165.44	118.12	38.13	19.83	11.16
Dinner	986.99	744.60	1,130.06	1,321.87	1,090.03	918.53	737.54	458.11
At fast-food restaurants*	331.42	332.68	421.32	499.01	368.08	263.55	158.40	100.14
At full-service restaurants	645.44	372.23	698.48	811.09	713.77	648.73	573.81	355.07
At vending machines, mobile vendors	2.86	3.19	4.54	5.39	2.58	1.21	1.62	–
At employer and school cafeterias	7.27	36.51	5.71	6.38	5.59	5.04	3.71	2.90
Snacks and nonalcoholic beverages	155.29	163.19	186.12	216.54	172.36	141.60	87.12	45.42
At fast-food restaurants*	102.25	91.26	122.66	154.03	110.82	91.71	56.82	29.06
At full-service restaurants	28.53	31.02	33.85	26.10	33.37	31.81	21.85	12.52
At vending machines, mobile vendors	18.59	32.53	21.38	24.35	23.34	14.94	6.71	2.78
At employer and school cafeterias	5.93	8.38	8.23	12.06	4.83	3.15	1.73	1.06
Breakfast and brunch	212.05	159.50	243.83	239.76	242.10	190.23	197.10	131.56
At fast-food restaurants*	110.61	78.54	147.30	135.76	125.16	94.42	90.36	42.16
At full-service restaurants	84.81	57.30	79.52	86.66	87.42	85.26	100.00	85.96
At vending machines, mobile vendors	3.21	6.26	2.28	3.76	4.01	2.76	2.85	1.13
At employer and school cafeterias	13.42	17.40	14.73	13.58	25.52	7.80	3.89	2.30
Restaurant and carry-out food on trips	223.08	82.60	171.66	240.46	271.80	269.45	272.54	130.35

* The category fast-food restaurants also includes take-out, delivery, concession stands, buffets, and cafeterias other than employer and school.
Note: "–" means sample is too small to make a reliable estimate.
Source: Bureau of Labor Statistics, unpublished tables from the 2010 Consumer Expenditure Survey

Table 5. Restaurants and Carry-Outs: Indexed spending by age, 2010

(indexed average annual spending of consumer units on restaurant and carry-out food, by age of consumer unit reference person, 2010; index definition: an index of 100 is the average for all consumer units; an index of 125 means that spending by consumer units in that group is 25 percent above the average for all consumer units; an index of 75 indicates spending that is 25 percent below the average for all consumer units)

	total consumer units	under 25	25 to 34	35 to 44	45 to 54	55 to 64	65 to 74	75+
Average spending of consumer units, total	$48,109	$27,483	$46,618	$55,946	$57,788	$50,900	$41,434	$31,529
Average spending of consumer units, index	100	57	97	116	120	106	86	66
RESTAURANTS AND CARRY-OUTS	100	75	110	129	111	95	82	53
Lunch	100	80	110	132	106	92	80	62
At fast-food restaurants*	100	88	127	134	108	92	63	37
At full-service restaurants	100	62	95	109	94	103	120	106
At vending machines, mobile vendors	100	132	123	120	117	101	26	43
At employer and school cafeterias	100	105	89	201	144	46	24	14
Dinner	100	75	115	134	110	93	75	46
At fast-food restaurants*	100	100	127	151	111	80	48	30
At full-service restaurants	100	58	108	126	111	101	89	55
At vending machines, mobile vendors	100	112	159	189	90	42	57	–
At employer and school cafeterias	100	502	79	88	77	69	51	40
Snacks and nonalcoholic beverages	100	105	120	139	111	91	56	29
At fast-food restaurants*	100	89	120	151	108	90	56	28
At full-service restaurants	100	109	119	92	117	112	77	44
At vending machines, mobile vendors	100	175	115	131	126	80	36	15
At employer and school cafeterias	100	141	139	203	82	53	29	18
Breakfast and brunch	100	75	115	113	114	90	93	62
At fast-food restaurants*	100	71	133	123	113	85	82	38
At full-service restaurants	100	68	94	102	103	101	118	101
At vending machines, mobile vendors	100	195	71	117	125	86	89	35
At employer and school cafeterias	100	130	110	101	190	58	29	17
Restaurant and carry-out food on trips	100	37	77	108	122	121	122	58

* The category fast-food restaurants also includes take-out, delivery, concession stands, buffets, and cafeterias other than employer and school.
Note: "–" means sample is too small to make a reliable estimate.
Source: Calculations by New Strategist based on the Bureau of Labor Statistics' 2010 Consumer Expenditure Survey

Table 6. Restaurants and Carry-Outs: Total spending by age, 2010

(total annual spending on restaurant and carry-out food, by consumer unit age group, 2010; consumer units and dollars in thousands)

	total consumer units	under 25	25 to 34	35 to 44	45 to 54	55 to 64	65 to 74	75+
Number of consumer units	121,107	8,034	20,166	21,912	25,054	21,359	13,031	11,551
Total spending of all consumer units	$5,826,317,286	$220,796,574	$940,088,102	$1,225,881,521	$1,447,826,816	$1,087,167,333	$539,924,499	$364,186,281
RESTAURANTS AND CARRY-OUTS	279,032,950	13,914,888	51,017,963	65,167,822	63,872,668	46,669,201	24,464,790	14,002,931
Lunch	87,997,557	4,676,672	16,097,106	20,935,601	19,369,498	14,207,580	7,598,767	5,161,333
At fast-food restaurants*	42,554,578	2,489,817	8,976,895	10,298,640	9,499,976	6,930,355	2,864,344	1,512,026
At full-service restaurants	34,533,661	1,407,959	5,444,820	6,802,580	6,677,643	6,291,294	4,448,783	3,481,240
At vending machines, mobile vendors	961,590	84,116	197,627	209,260	232,501	171,726	27,105	39,158
At employer and school cafeterias	9,947,729	694,700	1,477,966	3,625,121	2,959,379	814,419	258,405	128,909
Dinner	119,531,398	5,982,116	22,788,790	28,964,815	27,309,612	19,618,882	9,610,884	5,291,629
At fast-food restaurants*	40,137,282	2,672,751	8,496,339	10,934,307	9,221,876	5,629,165	2,064,110	1,156,717
At full-service restaurants	78,167,302	2,990,496	14,085,548	17,772,604	17,882,794	13,856,224	7,477,318	4,101,414
At vending machines, mobile vendors	346,366	25,629	91,554	118,106	64,639	25,844	21,110	–
At employer and school cafeterias	880,448	293,321	115,148	139,799	140,052	107,649	48,345	33,498
Snacks and nonalcoholic beverages	18,806,706	1,311,069	3,753,296	4,744,825	4,318,307	3,024,434	1,135,261	524,646
At fast-food restaurants*	12,383,191	733,183	2,473,562	3,375,105	2,776,484	1,958,834	740,421	335,672
At full-service restaurants	3,455,183	249,215	682,619	571,903	836,052	679,430	284,727	144,619
At vending machines, mobile vendors	2,251,379	261,346	431,149	533,557	584,760	319,104	87,438	32,112
At employer and school cafeterias	718,165	67,325	165,966	264,259	121,011	67,281	22,544	12,244
Breakfast and brunch	25,680,739	1,281,423	4,917,076	5,253,621	6,065,573	4,063,123	2,568,410	1,519,650
At fast-food restaurants*	13,395,645	630,990	2,970,452	2,974,773	3,135,759	2,016,717	1,177,481	486,990
At full-service restaurants	10,271,085	460,348	1,603,600	1,898,894	2,190,221	1,821,068	1,303,100	992,924
At vending machines, mobile vendors	388,754	50,293	45,979	82,389	100,467	58,951	37,138	13,053
At employer and school cafeterias	1,625,256	139,792	297,045	297,565	639,378	166,600	50,691	26,567
Restaurant and carry-out food on trips	27,016,550	663,608	3,461,696	5,268,960	6,809,677	5,755,183	3,551,469	1,505,673

* The category fast-food restaurants also includes take-out, delivery, concession stands, buffets, and cafeterias other than employer and school.
Note: Numbers may not add to total because of rounding. "–" means sample is too small to make a reliable estimate.
Source: Calculations by New Strategist based on the Bureau of Labor Statistics' 2010 Consumer Expenditure Survey

Table 7. Restaurants and Carry-Outs: Market shares by age, 2010

(percentage of total annual spending on restaurant and carry-out food accounted for by consumer unit age groups, 2010)

	total consumer units	under 25	25 to 34	35 to 44	45 to 54	55 to 64	65 to 74	75+
Share of total consumer units	100.0%	6.6%	16.7%	18.1%	20.7%	17.6%	10.8%	9.5%
Share of total before-tax income	100.0	2.9	15.9	22.0	26.4	19.5	8.6	4.9
Share of total spending	100.0	3.8	16.1	21.0	24.8	18.7	9.3	6.3
RESTAURANTS AND CARRY-OUTS	100.0	5.0	18.3	23.4	22.9	16.7	8.8	5.0
Lunch	100.0	5.3	18.3	23.8	22.0	16.1	8.6	5.9
At fast-food restaurants*	100.0	5.9	21.1	24.2	22.3	16.3	6.7	3.6
At full-service restaurants	100.0	4.1	15.8	19.7	19.3	18.2	12.9	10.1
At vending machines, mobile vendors	100.0	8.7	20.6	21.8	24.2	17.9	2.8	4.1
At employer and school cafeterias	100.0	7.0	14.9	36.4	29.7	8.2	2.6	1.3
Dinner	100.0	5.0	19.1	24.2	22.8	16.4	8.0	4.4
At fast-food restaurants*	100.0	6.7	21.2	27.2	23.0	14.0	5.1	2.9
At full-service restaurants	100.0	3.8	18.0	22.7	22.9	17.7	9.6	5.2
At vending machines, mobile vendors	100.0	7.4	26.4	34.1	18.7	7.5	6.1	–
At employer and school cafeterias	100.0	33.3	13.1	15.9	15.9	12.2	5.5	3.8
Snacks and nonalcoholic beverages	100.0	7.0	20.0	25.2	23.0	16.1	6.0	2.8
At fast-food restaurants*	100.0	5.9	20.0	27.3	22.4	15.8	6.0	2.7
At full-service restaurants	100.0	7.2	19.8	16.6	24.2	19.7	8.2	4.2
At vending machines, mobile vendors	100.0	11.6	19.2	23.7	26.0	14.2	3.9	1.4
At employer and school cafeterias	100.0	9.4	23.1	36.8	16.9	9.4	3.1	1.7
Breakfast and brunch	100.0	5.0	19.1	20.5	23.6	15.8	10.0	5.9
At fast-food restaurants*	100.0	4.7	22.2	22.2	23.4	15.1	8.8	3.6
At full-service restaurants	100.0	4.5	15.6	18.5	21.3	17.7	12.7	9.7
At vending machines, mobile vendors	100.0	12.9	11.8	21.2	25.8	15.2	9.6	3.4
At employer and school cafeterias	100.0	8.6	18.3	18.3	39.3	10.3	3.1	1.6
Restaurant and carry-out food on trips	100.0	2.5	12.8	19.5	25.2	21.3	13.1	5.6

* The category fast-food restaurants also includes take-out, delivery, concession stands, buffets, and cafeterias other than employer and school.
Note: Numbers may not add to total because of rounding. "–" means sample is too small to make a reliable estimate.
Source: Calculations by New Strategist based on the Bureau of Labor Statistics' 2010 Consumer Expenditure Survey

Table 8. Restaurants and Carry-Outs: Average spending by income, 2010

(average annual spending on restaurant and carry-out food, by before-tax income of consumer units, 2010)

	total consumer units	under $20,000	$20,000–$39,999	$40,000–$49,999	$50,000–$69,999	$70,000–$79,999	$80,000–$99,999	$100,000 or more
Number of consumer units (in 000s)	121,107	26,429	27,751	11,446	17,368	7,250	10,098	20,766
Number of persons per consumer unit	2.5	1.7	2.3	2.6	2.8	2.9	3.0	3.2
Average before-tax income of consumer units	$62,481.00	$10,691.03	$29,581.29	$44,734.00	$59,253.00	$74,602.00	$89,140.00	$167,651.00
Average spending of consumer units, total	48,108.84	21,296.16	32,160.45	40,616.28	47,965.65	57,024.31	62,966.34	97,737.31
RESTAURANTS AND CARRY-OUTS	**2,304.02**	**980.11**	**1,424.49**	**2,006.62**	**2,436.52**	**2,919.67**	**3,033.00**	**4,716.06**
Lunch	**726.61**	**351.12**	**477.30**	**653.53**	**766.68**	**948.44**	**960.05**	**1,372.29**
At fast-food restaurants*	351.38	188.32	246.94	346.74	377.68	445.83	469.75	592.26
At full-service restaurants	285.15	128.68	171.87	238.32	273.38	429.54	356.64	597.91
At vending machines, mobile vendors	7.94	3.47	7.02	10.33	8.89	11.86	11.66	9.32
At employer and school cafeterias	82.14	30.65	51.47	58.14	106.73	61.21	122.00	172.79
Dinner	**986.99**	**397.44**	**590.36**	**870.15**	**1,034.07**	**1,256.18**	**1,300.73**	**2,085.99**
At fast-food restaurants*	331.42	175.02	231.57	344.92	372.31	412.55	429.80	550.08
At full-service restaurants	645.44	208.42	349.73	514.37	653.92	835.13	859.48	1,525.93
At vending machines, mobile vendors	2.86	1.03	3.92	2.72	4.14	3.74	0.63	3.40
At employer and school cafeterias	7.27	12.98	5.13	8.13	3.70	4.75	10.82	6.57
Snacks and nonalcoholic beverages	**155.29**	**72.14**	**107.18**	**129.13**	**170.95**	**208.36**	**191.59**	**296.51**
At fast-food restaurants*	102.25	44.56	63.29	83.63	117.67	135.44	129.10	204.18
At full-service restaurants	28.53	10.86	21.68	18.45	30.91	37.42	32.54	59.97
At vending machines, mobile vendors	18.59	13.70	17.54	22.16	17.79	19.81	20.29	24.16
At employer and school cafeterias	5.93	3.01	4.68	4.89	4.57	15.70	9.66	8.20
Breakfast and brunch	**212.05**	**109.88**	**151.65**	**214.35**	**241.95**	**250.89**	**286.75**	**349.77**
At fast-food restaurants*	110.61	61.97	85.62	112.10	114.92	133.19	146.39	177.29
At full-service restaurants	84.81	35.14	56.83	81.96	105.51	104.12	116.98	147.81
At vending machines, mobile vendors	3.21	2.40	1.91	3.98	3.00	4.41	4.12	5.25
At employer and school cafeterias	13.42	10.37	7.29	16.31	18.51	9.17	19.26	19.43
Restaurant and carry-out food on trips	**223.08**	**49.53**	**98.01**	**139.46**	**222.87**	**255.80**	**293.88**	**611.50**

* The category fast-food restaurants also includes take-out, delivery, concession stands, buffets, and cafeterias other than employer and school.
Source: Bureau of Labor Statistics, unpublished tables from the 2010 Consumer Expenditure Survey

Table 9.   Restaurants and Carry-Outs: Indexed spending by income, 2010

(indexed average annual spending of consumer units on restaurant and carry-out food, by before-tax income of consumer unit, 2010; index definition: an index of 100 is the average for all consumer units; an index of 125 means that spending by consumer units in that group is 25 percent above the average for all consumer units; an index of 75 indicates spending that is 25 percent below the average for all consumer units)

	total consumer units	under $20,000	$20,000–$39,999	$40,000–$49,999	$50,000–$69,999	$70,000–$79,999	$80,000–$99,999	$100,000 or more
Average spending of consumer units, total	$48,109	$21,296	$32,160	$40,616	$47,966	$57,024	$62,966	$97,737
Average spending of consumer units, index	100	44	67	84	100	119	131	203
RESTAURANTS AND CARRY-OUTS	100	43	62	87	106	127	132	205
Lunch	100	48	66	90	106	131	132	189
At fast-food restaurants*	100	54	70	99	108	127	134	169
At full-service restaurants	100	45	60	84	96	151	125	210
At vending machines, mobile vendors	100	44	89	130	112	149	147	117
At employer and school cafeterias	100	37	63	71	130	75	149	210
Dinner	100	40	60	88	105	127	132	211
At fast-food restaurants*	100	53	70	104	112	125	130	166
At full-service restaurants	100	32	54	80	101	129	133	236
At vending machines, mobile vendors	100	36	137	95	145	131	22	119
At employer and school cafeterias	100	179	71	112	51	65	149	90
Snacks and nonalcoholic beverages	100	47	69	83	110	134	123	191
At fast-food restaurants*	100	44	62	82	115	133	126	200
At full-service restaurants	100	38	76	65	108	131	114	210
At vending machines, mobile vendors	100	74	94	119	96	107	109	130
At employer and school cafeterias	100	51	79	83	77	265	163	138
Breakfast and brunch	100	52	72	101	114	118	135	165
At fast-food restaurants*	100	56	77	101	104	120	132	160
At full-service restaurants	100	41	67	97	124	123	138	174
At vending machines, mobile vendors	100	75	60	124	94	137	128	164
At employer and school cafeterias	100	77	54	122	138	68	144	145
Restaurant and carry-out food on trips	100	22	44	63	100	115	132	274

* The category fast-food restaurants also includes take-out, delivery, concession stands, buffets, and cafeterias other than employer and school.
Source: Calculations by New Strategist based on the Bureau of Labor Statistics' 2010 Consumer Expenditure Survey

Table 10.   Restaurants and Carry-Outs: Total spending by income, 2010

(total annual spending on restaurant and carry-out food, by before-tax income group of consumer units, 2010; consumer units and dollars in thousands)

	total consumer units	under $20,000	$20,000– $39,999	$40,000– $49,999	$50,000– $69,999	$70,000– $79,999	$80,000– $99,999	$100,000 or more
Number of consumer units	121,107	26,429	27,751	11,446	17,368	7,250	10,098	20,766
Total spending of all consumer units	$5,826,317,286	$562,836,095	$892,484,515	$464,893,941	$833,067,409	$413,426,248	$635,834,101	$2,029,612,980
RESTAURANTS AND CARRY-OUTS	**279,032,950**	**25,903,297**	**39,531,159**	**22,967,773**	**42,317,479**	**21,167,608**	**30,627,234**	**97,933,702**
Lunch	**87,997,557**	**9,279,677**	**13,245,491**	**7,480,304**	**13,315,698**	**6,876,190**	**9,694,585**	**28,496,974**
At fast-food restaurants*	42,554,578	4,977,130	6,852,705	3,968,786	6,559,546	3,232,268	4,743,536	12,298,871
At full-service restaurants	34,533,661	3,400,919	4,769,538	2,727,811	4,748,064	3,114,165	3,601,351	12,416,199
At vending machines, mobile vendors	961,590	91,713	194,924	118,237	154,402	85,985	117,743	193,539
At employer and school cafeterias	9,947,729	810,079	1,428,325	665,470	1,853,687	443,773	1,231,956	3,588,157
Dinner	**119,531,398**	**10,503,934**	**16,383,006**	**9,959,737**	**17,959,728**	**9,107,305**	**13,134,772**	**43,317,668**
At fast-food restaurants*	40,137,282	4,625,506	6,426,272	3,947,954	6,466,280	2,990,988	4,340,120	11,422,961
At full-service restaurants	78,167,302	5,508,419	9,705,418	5,887,479	11,357,283	6,054,693	8,679,029	31,687,462
At vending machines, mobile vendors	346,366	27,185	108,848	31,133	71,904	27,115	6,362	70,604
At employer and school cafeterias	880,448	342,937	142,468	93,056	64,262	34,438	109,260	136,433
Snacks and nonalcoholic beverages	**18,806,706**	**1,906,590**	**2,974,408**	**1,478,022**	**2,969,060**	**1,510,610**	**1,934,676**	**6,157,327**
At fast-food restaurants*	12,383,191	1,177,745	1,756,396	957,229	2,043,693	981,940	1,303,652	4,240,002
At full-service restaurants	3,455,183	287,120	601,725	211,179	536,845	271,295	328,589	1,245,337
At vending machines, mobile vendors	2,251,379	362,115	486,648	253,643	308,977	143,623	204,888	501,707
At employer and school cafeterias	718,165	79,610	129,786	55,971	79,372	113,825	97,547	170,281
Breakfast and brunch	**25,680,739**	**2,904,030**	**4,208,349**	**2,453,450**	**4,202,188**	**1,818,953**	**2,895,602**	**7,263,324**
At fast-food restaurants*	13,395,645	1,637,839	2,376,052	1,283,097	1,995,931	965,628	1,478,246	3,681,604
At full-service restaurants	10,271,085	928,669	1,577,159	938,114	1,832,498	754,870	1,181,264	3,069,423
At vending machines, mobile vendors	388,754	63,499	53,049	45,555	52,104	31,973	41,604	109,022
At employer and school cafeterias	1,625,256	273,970	202,236	186,684	321,482	66,483	194,488	403,483
Restaurant and carry-out food on trips	**27,016,550**	**1,309,067**	**2,719,905**	**1,596,259**	**3,870,806**	**1,854,550**	**2,967,600**	**12,698,409**

* The category fast-food restaurants also includes take-out, delivery, concession stands, buffets, and cafeterias other than employer and school.
Note: Numbers may not add to total because of rounding.
Source: Calculations by New Strategist based on the Bureau of Labor Statistics' 2010 Consumer Expenditure Survey

Table 11. Restaurants and Carry-Outs: Market shares by income, 2010

(percentage of total annual spending on restaurant and carry-out food accounted for by before-tax income group of consumer units, 2010)

	total consumer units	under $20,000	$20,000–$39,999	$40,000–$49,999	$50,000–$69,999	$70,000–$79,999	$80,000–$99,999	$100,000 or more
Share of total consumer units	100.0%	21.8%	22.9%	9.5%	14.3%	6.0%	8.3%	17.1%
Share of total before-tax income	100.0	3.7	10.8	6.8	13.6	7.1	11.9	46.0
Share of total spending	100.0	9.7	15.3	8.0	14.3	7.1	10.9	34.8
RESTAURANTS AND CARRY-OUTS	100.0	9.3	14.2	8.2	15.2	7.6	11.0	35.1
Lunch	100.0	10.5	15.1	8.5	15.1	7.8	11.0	32.4
At fast-food restaurants*	100.0	11.7	16.1	9.3	15.4	7.6	11.1	28.9
At full-service restaurants	100.0	9.8	13.8	7.9	13.7	9.0	10.4	36.0
At vending machines, mobile vendors	100.0	9.5	20.3	12.3	16.1	8.9	12.2	20.1
At employer and school cafeterias	100.0	8.1	14.4	6.7	18.6	4.5	12.4	36.1
Dinner	100.0	8.8	13.7	8.3	15.0	7.6	11.0	36.2
At fast-food restaurants*	100.0	11.5	16.0	9.8	16.1	7.5	10.8	28.5
At full-service restaurants	100.0	7.1	12.4	7.5	14.5	7.7	11.1	40.5
At vending machines, mobile vendors	100.0	7.8	31.4	9.0	20.8	7.8	1.8	20.4
At employer and school cafeterias	100.0	39.0	16.2	10.6	7.3	3.9	12.4	15.5
Snacks and nonalcoholic beverages	100.0	10.1	15.8	7.9	15.8	8.0	10.3	32.7
At fast-food restaurants*	100.0	9.5	14.2	7.7	16.5	7.9	10.5	34.2
At full-service restaurants	100.0	8.3	17.4	6.1	15.5	7.9	9.5	36.0
At vending machines, mobile vendors	100.0	16.1	21.6	11.3	13.7	6.4	9.1	22.3
At employer and school cafeterias	100.0	11.1	18.1	7.8	11.1	15.8	13.6	23.7
Breakfast and brunch	100.0	11.3	16.4	9.6	16.4	7.1	11.3	28.3
At fast-food restaurants*	100.0	12.2	17.7	9.6	14.9	7.2	11.0	27.5
At full-service restaurants	100.0	9.0	15.4	9.1	17.8	7.3	11.5	29.9
At vending machines, mobile vendors	100.0	16.3	13.6	11.7	13.4	8.2	10.7	28.0
At employer and school cafeterias	100.0	16.9	12.4	11.5	19.8	4.1	12.0	24.8
Restaurant and carry-out food on trips	100.0	4.8	10.1	5.9	14.3	6.9	11.0	47.0

* The category fast-food restaurants also includes take-out, delivery, concession stands, buffets, and cafeterias other than employer and school.
Note: Numbers may not add to total because of rounding.
Source: Calculations by New Strategist based on the Bureau of Labor Statistics' 2010 Consumer Expenditure Survey

Table 12. Restaurants and Carry-Outs: Average spending by high-income consumer units, 2010

(average annual spending on restaurant and carry-out food, by before-tax income of consumer units with high incomes, 2010)

	total consumer units	$100,000 or more	$100,000–$119,999	$120,000–$149,999	$150,000 or more
Number of consumer units (in 000s)	121,107	20,766	6,749	5,865	8,151
Number of persons per consumer unit	2.5	3.2	3.1	3.2	3.2
Average before-tax income of consumer units	$62,481.00	$167,651.00	$108,503.00	$132,750.00	$241,739.00
Average spending of consumer units, total	48,108.84	97,737.31	74,797.40	89,613.76	123,063.97
RESTAURANTS AND CARRY-OUTS	**2,304.02**	**4,716.06**	**3,855.22**	**4,295.39**	**5,819.30**
Lunch	**726.61**	**1,372.29**	**1,192.52**	**1,280.80**	**1,610.23**
At fast-food restaurants*	351.38	592.26	493.68	660.24	635.38
At full-service restaurants	285.15	597.91	536.22	477.19	745.62
At vending machines, mobile vendors	7.94	9.32	11.60	12.47	4.82
At employer and school cafeterias	82.14	172.79	151.01	130.90	224.41
Dinner	**986.99**	**2,085.99**	**1,681.00**	**1,831.80**	**2,657.61**
At fast-food restaurants*	331.42	550.08	487.95	536.41	619.05
At full-service restaurants	645.44	1,525.93	1,180.75	1,291.40	2,026.36
At vending machines, mobile vendors	2.86	3.40	4.46	0.99	4.18
At employer and school cafeterias	7.27	6.57	7.83	3.00	8.02
Snacks and nonalcoholic beverages	**155.29**	**296.51**	**246.84**	**282.52**	**353.91**
At fast-food restaurants*	102.25	204.18	172.88	200.97	236.19
At full-service restaurants	28.53	59.97	46.66	50.84	79.34
At vending machines, mobile vendors	18.59	24.16	24.27	22.64	25.18
At employer and school cafeterias	5.93	8.20	3.03	8.06	13.21
Breakfast and brunch	**212.05**	**349.77**	**302.18**	**387.63**	**366.85**
At fast-food restaurants*	110.61	177.29	160.54	208.94	169.75
At full-service restaurants	84.81	147.81	115.67	148.68	177.61
At vending machines, mobile vendors	3.21	5.25	9.48	3.36	2.63
At employer and school cafeterias	13.42	19.43	16.49	26.66	16.86
Restaurant and carry-out food on trips	**223.08**	**611.50**	**432.68**	**512.64**	**830.70**

* The category fast-food restaurants also includes take-out, delivery, concession stands, buffets, and cafeterias other than employer and school.
Source: Bureau of Labor Statistics, unpublished tables from the 2010 Consumer Expenditure Survey

Table 13.   Restaurants and Carry-Outs: Indexed spending by high-income consumer units, 2010

(indexed average annual spending of consumer units with high incomes on restaurant and carry-out food, by before-tax income of consumer unit, 2010; index definition: an index of 100 is the average for all consumer units; an index of 125 means that spending by consumer units in that group is 25 percent above the average for all consumer units; an index of 75 indicates spending that is 25 percent below the average for all consumer units)

	total consumer units	$100,000 or more	$100,000– $119,999	$120,000– $149,999	$150,000 or more
Average spending of consumer units, total	$48,109	$97,737	$74,797	$89,614	$123,064
Average spending of consumer units, index	100	203	156	186	256
RESTAURANTS AND CARRY-OUTS	100	205	167	186	253
Lunch	100	189	164	176	222
At fast-food restaurants*	100	169	141	188	181
At full-service restaurants	100	210	188	167	262
At vending machines, mobile vendors	100	117	146	157	61
At employer and school cafeterias	100	210	184	159	273
Dinner	100	211	170	186	269
At fast-food restaurants*	100	166	147	162	187
At full-service restaurants	100	236	183	200	314
At vending machines, mobile vendors	100	119	156	35	146
At employer and school cafeterias	100	90	108	41	110
Snacks and nonalcoholic beverages	100	191	159	182	228
At fast-food restaurants*	100	200	169	197	231
At full-service restaurants	100	210	164	178	278
At vending machines, mobile vendors	100	130	131	122	135
At employer and school cafeterias	100	138	51	136	223
Breakfast and brunch	100	165	143	183	173
At fast-food restaurants*	100	160	145	189	154
At full-service restaurants	100	174	136	175	209
At vending machines, mobile vendors	100	164	295	105	82
At employer and school cafeterias	100	145	123	199	126
Restaurant and carry-out food on trips	100	274	194	230	372

* The category fast-food restaurants also includes take-out, delivery, concession stands, buffets, and cafeterias other than employer and school.
Source: Calculations by New Strategist based on the Bureau of Labor Statistics' 2010 Consumer Expenditure Survey

Table 14. Restaurants and Carry-Outs: Total spending by high-income consumer units, 2010

(total annual spending on restaurant and carry-out food, by before-tax income group of consumer units with high incomes, 2010; consumer units and dollars in thousands)

	total consumer units	$100,000 or more	$100,000– $119,999	$120,000– $149,999	$150,000 or more
Number of consumer units	121,107	20,766	6,749	5,865	8,151
Total spending of all consumer units	$5,826,317,286	$2,029,612,980	$504,807,653	$525,584,702	$1,003,094,420
RESTAURANTS AND CARRY-OUTS	279,032,950	97,933,702	26,018,880	25,192,462	47,433,114
Lunch	87,997,557	28,496,974	8,048,318	7,511,892	13,124,985
At fast-food restaurants*	42,554,578	12,298,871	3,331,846	3,872,308	5,178,982
At full-service restaurants	34,533,661	12,416,199	3,618,949	2,798,719	6,077,549
At vending machines, mobile vendors	961,590	193,539	78,288	73,137	39,288
At employer and school cafeterias	9,947,729	3,588,157	1,019,167	767,729	1,829,166
Dinner	119,531,398	43,317,668	11,345,069	10,743,507	21,662,179
At fast-food restaurants*	40,137,282	11,422,961	3,293,175	3,146,045	5,045,877
At full-service restaurants	78,167,302	31,687,462	7,968,882	7,574,061	16,516,860
At vending machines, mobile vendors	346,366	70,604	30,101	5,806	34,071
At employer and school cafeterias	880,448	136,433	52,845	17,595	65,371
Snacks and nonalcoholic beverages	18,806,706	6,157,327	1,665,923	1,656,980	2,884,720
At fast-food restaurants*	12,383,191	4,240,002	1,166,767	1,178,689	1,925,185
At full-service restaurants	3,455,183	1,245,337	314,908	298,177	646,700
At vending machines, mobile vendors	2,251,379	501,707	163,798	132,784	205,242
At employer and school cafeterias	718,165	170,281	20,450	47,272	107,675
Breakfast and brunch	25,680,739	7,263,324	2,039,413	2,273,450	2,990,194
At fast-food restaurants*	13,395,645	3,681,604	1,083,485	1,225,433	1,383,632
At full-service restaurants	10,271,085	3,069,423	780,657	872,008	1,447,699
At vending machines, mobile vendors	388,754	109,022	63,981	19,706	21,437
At employer and school cafeterias	1,625,256	403,483	111,291	156,361	137,426
Restaurant and carry-out food on trips	27,016,550	12,698,409	2,920,157	3,006,634	6,771,036

* The category fast-food restaurants also includes take-out, delivery, concession stands, buffets, and cafeterias other than employer and school.

Note: Numbers may not add to total because of rounding.

Source: Calculations by New Strategist based on the Bureau of Labor Statistics' 2010 Consumer Expenditure Survey

Table 15. Restaurants and Carry-Outs: Market shares by high-income consumer units, 2010

(percentage of total annual spending on restaurant and carry-out food accounted for by before-tax income group of consumer units with high incomes, 2010)

	total consumer units	$100,000 or more	$100,000– $119,999	$120,000– $149,999	$150,000 or more
Share of total consumer units	100.0%	17.1%	5.6%	4.8%	6.7%
Share of total before-tax income	100.0	46.0	9.7	10.3	26.0
Share of total spending	100.0	34.8	8.7	9.0	17.2
RESTAURANTS AND CARRY-OUTS	100.0	35.1	9.3	9.0	17.0
Lunch	100.0	32.4	9.1	8.5	14.9
At fast-food restaurants*	100.0	28.9	7.8	9.1	12.2
At full-service restaurants	100.0	36.0	10.5	8.1	17.6
At vending machines, mobile vendors	100.0	20.1	8.1	7.6	4.1
At employer and school cafeterias	100.0	36.1	10.2	7.7	18.4
Dinner	100.0	36.2	9.5	9.0	18.1
At fast-food restaurants*	100.0	28.5	8.2	7.8	12.6
At full-service restaurants	100.0	40.5	10.2	9.7	21.1
At vending machines, mobile vendors	100.0	20.4	8.7	1.7	9.8
At employer and school cafeterias	100.0	15.5	6.0	2.0	7.4
Snacks and nonalcoholic beverages	100.0	32.7	8.9	8.8	15.3
At fast-food restaurants*	100.0	34.2	9.4	9.5	15.5
At full-service restaurants	100.0	36.0	9.1	8.6	18.7
At vending machines, mobile vendors	100.0	22.3	7.3	5.9	9.1
At employer and school cafeterias	100.0	23.7	2.8	6.6	15.0
Breakfast and brunch	100.0	28.3	7.9	8.9	11.6
At fast-food restaurants*	100.0	27.5	8.1	9.1	10.3
At full-service restaurants	100.0	29.9	7.6	8.5	14.1
At vending machines, mobile vendors	100.0	28.0	16.5	5.1	5.5
At employer and school cafeterias	100.0	24.8	6.8	9.6	8.5
Restaurant and carry-out food on trips	100.0	47.0	10.8	11.1	25.1

* The category fast-food restaurants also includes take-out, delivery, concession stands, buffets, and cafeterias other than employer and school.
Note: Numbers may not add to total because of rounding.
Source: Calculations by New Strategist based on the Bureau of Labor Statistics' 2010 Consumer Expenditure Survey

Table 16. Restaurants and Carry-Outs: Average spending by household type, 2010

(average annual spending of consumer units (CU) on restaurant and carry-out food, by type of consumer unit, 2010)

| | total consumer units | total married couples | married couples, no children | married couples with children | | | | single parent, at least one child <18 | single person |
				total	oldest child under 6	oldest child 6 to 17	oldest child 18 or older		
Number of consumer units (in 000s)	121,107	59,739	25,723	28,172	5,185	14,242	8,745	7,141	35,479
Number of persons per CU	2.5	3.2	2.0	4.0	3.5	4.2	4.0	2.9	1.0
Average before-tax income of CU	$62,481.00	$85,296.00	$76,543.00	$93,627.00	$87,439.00	$94,807.00	$95,374.00	$34,652.00	$32,979.00
Average spending of CU, total	48,108.84	61,762.12	56,035.40	67,382.98	61,756.04	69,536.22	67,057.03	36,933.33	29,149.14
RESTAURANTS AND CARRY-OUTS	**2,304.02**	**2,864.67**	**2,510.74**	**3,192.70**	**2,625.88**	**3,438.95**	**3,117.04**	**1,723.18**	**1,499.23**
Lunch	**726.61**	**894.21**	**725.17**	**1,029.19**	**826.11**	**1,088.21**	**1,045.11**	**590.83**	**471.60**
At fast-food restaurants*	351.38	412.42	298.52	495.50	436.52	495.48	525.72	326.54	224.42
At full-service restaurants	285.15	370.96	389.77	357.49	324.18	370.81	354.67	88.02	208.77
At vending machines, mobile vendors	7.94	7.89	6.01	10.02	9.84	13.21	5.35	5.17	6.43
At employer and school cafeterias	82.14	102.94	30.87	166.18	55.57	208.71	159.38	171.11	31.99
Dinner	**986.99**	**1,220.64**	**1,066.40**	**1,374.91**	**1,220.02**	**1,461.11**	**1,325.68**	**714.32**	**644.89**
At fast-food restaurants*	331.42	403.38	269.44	509.83	450.83	541.20	493.24	382.03	180.10
At full-service restaurants	645.44	809.63	792.26	854.08	764.46	906.44	821.89	323.55	452.71
At vending machines, mobile vendors	2.86	2.90	1.77	3.93	1.40	5.30	3.18	1.57	1.37
At employer and school cafeterias	7.27	4.74	2.94	7.08	3.33	8.16	7.38	7.17	10.71
Snacks and nonalcoholic beverages	**155.29**	**188.68**	**134.02**	**239.75**	**193.77**	**264.25**	**226.75**	**121.51**	**101.04**
At fast-food restaurants*	102.25	131.22	87.52	170.88	149.97	189.15	154.34	78.08	55.38
At full-service restaurants	28.53	29.84	29.89	31.94	17.18	28.99	43.89	10.02	30.11
At vending machines, mobile vendors	18.59	20.27	13.11	25.24	18.34	28.83	23.43	26.92	12.14
At employer and school cafeterias	5.93	7.35	3.50	11.70	8.28	17.29	5.11	6.49	3.41
Breakfast and brunch	**212.05**	**238.81**	**220.89**	**243.51**	**177.31**	**273.22**	**233.08**	**180.33**	**161.24**
At fast-food restaurants*	110.61	121.92	99.91	138.08	116.48	147.02	135.80	96.76	84.15
At full-service restaurants	84.81	101.26	111.80	84.69	46.29	99.03	82.95	38.49	65.99
At vending machines, mobile vendors	3.21	3.45	2.58	3.19	2.60	4.38	1.73	1.99	2.64
At employer and school cafeterias	13.42	12.18	6.61	17.55	11.94	22.80	12.60	43.09	8.46
Restaurant and carry-out food on trips	**223.08**	**322.33**	**364.26**	**305.34**	**208.67**	**352.16**	**286.42**	**116.19**	**120.46**

* The category fast-food restaurants also includes take-out, delivery, concession stands, buffets, and cafeterias other than employer and school.
Source: Bureau of Labor Statistics, unpublished tables from the 2010 Consumer Expenditure Survey

Table 17.   Restaurants and Carry-Outs: Indexed spending by household type, 2010

(indexed average annual spending of consumer units (CU) on restaurant and carry-out food, by type of consumer unit, 2010; index definition: an index of 100 is the average for all consumer units; an index of 125 means that spending by consumer units in that group is 25 percent above the average for all consumer units; an index of 75 indicates spending that is 25 percent below the average for all consumer units)

| | total consumer units | total married couples | married couples, no children | married couples with children | | | | single parent, at least one child <18 | single person |
				total	oldest child under 6	oldest child 6 to 17	oldest child 18 or older		
Average spending of CU, total	$48,109	$61,762	$56,035	$67,383	$61,756	$69,536	$67,057	$36,933	$29,149
Average spending of CU, index	100	128	117	140	128	145	139	77	61
RESTAURANTS AND CARRY-OUTS	100	124	109	139	114	149	135	75	65
Lunch	100	123	100	142	114	150	144	81	65
At fast-food restaurants*	100	117	85	141	124	141	150	93	64
At full-service restaurants	100	130	137	125	114	130	124	31	73
At vending machines, mobile vendors	100	99	76	126	124	166	67	65	81
At employer and school cafeterias	100	125	38	202	68	254	194	208	39
Dinner	100	124	108	139	124	148	134	72	65
At fast-food restaurants*	100	122	81	154	136	163	149	115	54
At full-service restaurants	100	125	123	132	118	140	127	50	70
At vending machines, mobile vendors	100	101	62	137	49	185	111	55	48
At employer and school cafeterias	100	65	40	97	46	112	102	99	147
Snacks and nonalcoholic beverages	100	122	86	154	125	170	146	78	65
At fast-food restaurants*	100	128	86	167	147	185	151	76	54
At full-service restaurants	100	105	105	112	60	102	154	35	106
At vending machines, mobile vendors	100	109	71	136	99	155	126	145	65
At employer and school cafeterias	100	124	59	197	140	292	86	109	58
Breakfast and brunch	100	113	104	115	84	129	110	85	76
At fast-food restaurants*	100	110	90	125	105	133	123	88	76
At full-service restaurants	100	119	132	100	55	117	98	45	78
At vending machines, mobile vendors	100	108	80	99	81	136	54	62	82
At employer and school cafeterias	100	91	49	131	89	170	94	321	63
Restaurant and carry-out food on trips	100	145	163	137	94	158	128	52	54

* The category fast-food restaurants also includes take-out, delivery, concession stands, buffets, and cafeterias other than employer and school.
Source: Calculations by New Strategist based on the Bureau of Labor Statistics' 2010 Consumer Expenditure Survey

Table 18. Restaurants and Carry-Outs: Total spending by household type, 2010

(total annual spending on restaurant and carry-out food, by consumer unit (CU) type, 2010; consumer units and dollars in thousands)

	total consumer units	total married couples	married couples, no children	married couples with children total	oldest child under 6	oldest child 6 to 17	oldest child 18 or older	single parent, at least one child <18	single person
Number of consumer units	121,107	59,739	25,723	28,172	5,185	14,242	8,745	7,141	35,479
Total spending of all CUs	$5,826,317,286	$3,689,607,287	$1,441,398,594	$1,898,313,313	$320,205,067	$990,334,845	$586,413,727	$263,740,910	$1,034,182,338
RESTAURANTS AND CARRY-OUTS	**279,032,950**	**171,132,521**	**64,583,765**	**89,944,744**	**13,615,188**	**48,977,526**	**27,258,515**	**12,305,228**	**53,191,181**
Lunch	**87,997,557**	**53,419,211**	**18,653,548**	**28,994,341**	**4,283,380**	**15,498,287**	**9,139,487**	**4,219,117**	**16,731,896**
At fast-food restaurants*	42,554,578	24,637,558	7,678,830	13,959,226	2,263,356	7,056,626	4,597,421	2,331,822	7,962,197
At full-service restaurants	34,533,661	22,160,779	10,026,054	10,071,208	1,680,873	5,281,076	3,101,589	628,551	7,406,951
At vending machines, mobile vendors	961,590	471,341	154,595	282,283	51,020	188,137	46,786	36,919	228,130
At employer and school cafeterias	9,947,729	6,149,533	794,069	4,681,623	288,131	2,972,448	1,393,778	1,221,897	1,134,973
Dinner	**119,531,398**	**72,919,813**	**27,431,007**	**38,733,965**	**6,325,804**	**20,809,129**	**11,593,072**	**5,100,959**	**22,880,052**
At fast-food restaurants*	40,137,282	24,097,518	6,930,805	14,362,931	2,337,554	7,707,770	4,313,384	2,728,076	6,389,768
At full-service restaurants	78,167,302	48,366,487	20,379,304	24,061,142	3,963,725	12,909,519	7,187,428	2,310,471	16,061,698
At vending machines, mobile vendors	346,366	173,243	45,530	110,716	7,259	75,483	27,809	11,211	48,606
At employer and school cafeterias	880,448	283,163	75,626	199,458	17,266	116,215	64,538	51,201	379,980
Snacks and nonalcoholic beverages	**18,806,706**	**11,271,555**	**3,447,397**	**6,754,237**	**1,004,697**	**3,763,449**	**1,982,929**	**867,703**	**3,584,798**
At fast-food restaurants*	12,383,191	7,838,952	2,251,277	4,814,031	777,594	2,693,874	1,349,703	557,569	1,964,827
At full-service restaurants	3,455,183	1,782,612	768,861	899,814	89,078	412,876	383,818	71,553	1,068,273
At vending machines, mobile vendors	2,251,379	1,210,910	337,229	711,061	95,093	410,597	204,895	192,236	430,715
At employer and school cafeterias	718,165	439,082	90,031	329,612	42,932	246,244	44,687	46,345	120,983
Breakfast and brunch	**25,680,739**	**14,266,271**	**5,681,954**	**6,860,164**	**919,352**	**3,891,199**	**2,038,285**	**1,287,737**	**5,720,634**
At fast-food restaurants*	13,395,645	7,283,379	2,569,985	3,889,990	603,949	2,093,859	1,187,571	690,963	2,985,558
At full-service restaurants	10,271,085	6,049,171	2,875,831	2,385,887	240,014	1,410,385	725,398	274,857	2,341,259
At vending machines, mobile vendors	388,754	206,100	66,365	89,869	13,481	62,380	15,129	14,211	93,665
At employer and school cafeterias	1,625,256	727,621	170,029	494,419	61,909	324,718	110,187	307,706	300,152
Restaurant and carry-out food on trips	**27,016,550**	**19,255,672**	**9,369,860**	**8,602,039**	**1,081,954**	**5,015,463**	**2,504,743**	**829,713**	**4,273,800**

* The category fast-food restaurants also includes take-out, delivery, concession stands, buffets, and cafeterias other than employer and school.
Note: Numbers do not add to total because not all types of consumer units are shown.
Source: Calculations by New Strategist based on the Bureau of Labor Statistics' 2010 Consumer Expenditure Survey

Table 19.   Restaurants and Carry-Outs: Market shares by household type, 2010

(percentage of total annual spending on restaurant and carry-out food accounted for by types of consumer units, 2010)

	total consumer units	total married couples	married couples, no children	married couples with children				single parent, at least one child <18	single person
				total	oldest child under 6	oldest child 6 to 17	oldest child 18 or older		
Share of total consumer units	100.0%	49.3%	21.2%	23.3%	4.3%	11.8%	7.2%	5.9%	29.3%
Share of total before-tax income	100.0	67.3	26.0	34.9	6.0	17.8	11.0	3.3	15.5
Share of total spending	100.0	63.3	24.7	32.6	5.5	17.0	10.1	4.5	17.8
RESTAURANTS AND CARRY-OUTS	100.0	61.3	23.1	32.2	4.9	17.6	9.8	4.4	19.1
Lunch	100.0	60.7	21.2	32.9	4.9	17.6	10.4	4.8	19.0
At fast-food restaurants*	100.0	57.9	18.0	32.8	5.3	16.6	10.8	5.5	18.7
At full-service restaurants	100.0	64.2	29.0	29.2	4.9	15.3	9.0	1.8	21.4
At vending machines, mobile vendors	100.0	49.0	16.1	29.4	5.3	19.6	4.9	3.8	23.7
At employer and school cafeterias	100.0	61.8	8.0	47.1	2.9	29.9	14.0	12.3	11.4
Dinner	100.0	61.0	22.9	32.4	5.3	17.4	9.7	4.3	19.1
At fast-food restaurants*	100.0	60.0	17.3	35.8	5.8	19.2	10.7	6.8	15.9
At full-service restaurants	100.0	61.9	26.1	30.8	5.1	16.5	9.2	3.0	20.5
At vending machines, mobile vendors	100.0	50.0	13.1	32.0	2.1	21.8	8.0	3.2	14.0
At employer and school cafeterias	100.0	32.2	8.6	22.7	2.0	13.2	7.3	5.8	43.2
Snacks and nonalcoholic beverages	100.0	59.9	18.3	35.9	5.3	20.0	10.5	4.6	19.1
At fast-food restaurants*	100.0	63.3	18.2	38.9	6.3	21.8	10.9	4.5	15.9
At full-service restaurants	100.0	51.6	22.3	26.0	2.6	11.9	11.1	2.1	30.9
At vending machines, mobile vendors	100.0	53.8	15.0	31.6	4.2	18.2	9.1	8.5	19.1
At employer and school cafeterias	100.0	61.1	12.5	45.9	6.0	34.3	6.2	6.5	16.8
Breakfast and brunch	100.0	55.6	22.1	26.7	3.6	15.2	7.9	5.0	22.3
At fast-food restaurants*	100.0	54.4	19.2	29.0	4.5	15.6	8.9	5.2	22.3
At full-service restaurants	100.0	58.9	28.0	23.2	2.3	13.7	7.1	2.7	22.8
At vending machines, mobile vendors	100.0	53.0	17.1	23.1	3.5	16.1	3.9	3.7	24.1
At employer and school cafeterias	100.0	44.8	10.5	30.4	3.8	20.0	6.8	18.9	18.5
Restaurant and carry-out food on trips	100.0	71.3	34.7	31.8	4.0	18.6	9.3	3.1	15.8

* The category fast-food restaurants also includes take-out, delivery, concession stands, buffets, and cafeterias other than employer and school.
Note: Market shares by type of consumer unit do not add to total because not all types of consumer units are shown.
Source: Calculations by New Strategist based on the Bureau of Labor Statistics' 2010 Consumer Expenditure Survey

Table 20. Restaurants and Carry-Outs: Average spending by race and Hispanic origin, 2010

(average annual spending of consumer units on restaurant and carry-out food, by race and Hispanic origin of consumer unit reference person, 2010)

	total consumer units	Asian	black	Hispanic	non-Hispanic white and other
Number of consumer units (in 000s)	121,107	5,151	14,820	14,754	91,816
Number of persons per consumer unit	2.5	2.7	2.6	3.3	2.4
Average before-tax income of consumer units	$62,481.00	$85,316.00	$45,727.00	$49,845.00	$67,283.00
Average spending of consumer units, total	48,108.84	58,375.54	35,862.76	41,456.34	51,166.60
RESTAURANTS AND CARRY-OUTS	**2,304.02**	**3,278.31**	**1,614.02**	**2,278.48**	**2,418.94**
Lunch	**726.61**	**1,121.26**	**562.01**	**814.68**	**738.56**
At fast-food restaurants*	351.38	569.22	315.08	449.39	341.56
At full-service restaurants	285.15	394.72	161.35	262.50	308.23
At vending machines, mobile vendors	7.94	6.45	5.70	12.91	7.53
At employer and school cafeterias	82.14	150.87	79.88	89.89	81.24
Dinner	**986.99**	**1,416.50**	**667.36**	**910.53**	**1,049.98**
At fast-food restaurants*	331.42	373.80	361.28	399.30	316.34
At full-service restaurants	645.44	1,022.51	301.50	498.66	723.02
At vending machines, mobile vendors	2.86	1.78	1.31	7.65	2.35
At employer and school cafeterias	7.27	18.42	3.27	4.92	8.27
Snacks and nonalcoholic beverages	**155.29**	**197.99**	**109.82**	**165.37**	**160.82**
At fast-food restaurants*	102.25	127.59	74.75	107.11	105.75
At full-service restaurants	28.53	25.86	18.56	29.06	30.04
At vending machines, mobile vendors	18.59	28.30	13.31	23.46	18.65
At employer and school cafeterias	5.93	16.23	3.20	5.74	6.38
Breakfast and brunch	**212.05**	**227.46**	**182.72**	**251.36**	**211.05**
At fast-food restaurants*	110.61	119.81	119.19	141.42	104.77
At full-service restaurants	84.81	78.18	46.06	91.00	90.18
At vending machines, mobile vendors	3.21	6.18	2.58	5.65	2.93
At employer and school cafeterias	13.42	23.28	14.89	13.30	13.17
Restaurant and carry-out food on trips	**223.08**	**315.10**	**92.11**	**136.54**	**258.53**

The category fast-food restaurants also includes take-out, delivery, concession stands, buffets, and cafeterias other than employer and school.
Note: "Asian" and "black" include Hispanics and non-Hispanics who identify themselves as being of the respective race alone. "Hispanic" includes people of any race who identify themselves as Hispanic. "Other" includes people who identify themselves as non-Hispanic and as Alaska Native, American Indian, Asian (who are also included in the "Asian" column), Native Hawaiian or other Pacific Islander, as well as non-Hispanics reporting more than one race.
Source: Bureau of Labor Statistics, unpublished tables from the 2010 Consumer Expenditure Survey

Table 21. Restaurants and Carry-Outs: Indexed spending by race and Hispanic origin, 2010

(indexed average annual spending of consumer units on restaurant and carry-out food, by race and Hispanic origin of consumer unit reference person, 2010; index definition: an index of 100 is the average for all consumer units; an index of 125 means that spending by consumer units in that group is 25 percent above the average for all consumer units; an index of 75 indicates spending that is 25 percent below the average for all consumer units)

	total consumer units	Asian	black	Hispanic	non-Hispanic white and other
Average spending of consumer units, total	$48,109	$58,376	$35,863	$41,456	$51,167
Average spending of consumer units, index	100	121	75	86	106
RESTAURANTS AND CARRY-OUTS	100	142	70	99	105
Lunch	100	154	77	112	102
At fast-food restaurants*	100	162	90	128	97
At full-service restaurants	100	138	57	92	108
At vending machines, mobile vendors	100	81	72	163	95
At employer and school cafeterias	100	184	97	109	99
Dinner	100	144	68	92	106
At fast-food restaurants*	100	113	109	121	95
At full-service restaurants	100	158	47	77	112
At vending machines, mobile vendors	100	62	46	268	82
At employer and school cafeterias	100	253	45	68	114
Snacks and nonalcoholic beverages	100	128	71	107	104
At fast-food restaurants*	100	125	73	105	103
At full-service restaurants	100	91	65	102	105
At vending machines, mobile vendors	100	152	72	126	100
At employer and school cafeterias	100	274	54	97	108
Breakfast and brunch	100	107	86	119	100
At fast-food restaurants*	100	108	108	128	95
At full-service restaurants	100	92	54	107	106
At vending machines, mobile vendors	100	193	80	176	91
At employer and school cafeterias	100	174	111	99	98
Restaurant and carry-out food on trips	100	141	41	61	116

* The category fast-food restaurants also includes take-out, delivery, concession stands, buffets, and cafeterias other than employer and school.
Note: "Asian" and "black" include Hispanics and non-Hispanics who identify themselves as being of the respective race alone. "Hispanic" includes people of any race who identify themselves as Hispanic. "Other" includes people who identify themselves as non-Hispanic and as Alaska Native, American Indian, Asian (who are also included in the "Asian" column), Native Hawaiian or other Pacific Islander, as well as non-Hispanics reporting more than one race.
Source: Calculations by New Strategist based on the Bureau of Labor Statistics' 2010 Consumer Expenditure Survey

Table 22. Restaurants and Carry-Outs: Total spending by race and Hispanic origin, 2010

(total annual spending on restaurant and carry-out food, by consumer unit race and Hispanic origin groups, 2010; consumer units and dollars in thousands)

	total consumer units	Asian	black	Hispanic	non-Hispanic white and other
Number of consumer units	121,107	5,151	14,820	14,754	91,816
Total spending of all consumer units	$5,826,317,286	$300,692,407	$531,486,103	$611,646,840	$4,697,912,546
RESTAURANTS AND CARRY-OUTS	**279,032,950**	**16,886,575**	**23,919,776**	**33,616,694**	**222,097,395**
Lunch	**87,997,557**	**5,775,610**	**8,328,988**	**12,019,789**	**67,811,625**
At fast-food restaurants*	42,554,578	2,932,052	4,669,486	6,630,300	31,360,673
At full-service restaurants	34,533,661	2,033,203	2,391,207	3,872,925	28,300,446
At vending machines, mobile vendors	961,590	33,224	84,474	190,474	691,375
At employer and school cafeterias	9,947,729	777,131	1,183,822	1,326,237	7,459,132
Dinner	**119,531,398**	**7,296,392**	**9,890,275**	**13,433,960**	**96,404,964**
At fast-food restaurants*	40,137,282	1,925,444	5,354,170	5,891,272	29,045,073
At full-service restaurants	78,167,302	5,266,949	4,468,230	7,357,230	66,384,804
At vending machines, mobile vendors	346,366	9,169	19,414	112,868	215,768
At employer and school cafeterias	880,448	94,881	48,461	72,590	759,318
Snacks and nonalcoholic beverages	**18,806,706**	**1,019,847**	**1,627,532**	**2,439,869**	**14,765,849**
At fast-food restaurants*	12,383,191	657,216	1,107,795	1,580,301	9,709,542
At full-service restaurants	3,455,183	133,205	275,059	428,751	2,758,153
At vending machines, mobile vendors	2,251,379	145,773	197,254	346,129	1,712,368
At employer and school cafeterias	718,165	83,601	47,424	84,688	585,786
Breakfast and brunch	**25,680,739**	**1,171,647**	**2,707,910**	**3,708,565**	**19,377,767**
At fast-food restaurants*	13,395,645	617,141	1,766,396	2,086,511	9,619,562
At full-service restaurants	10,271,085	402,705	682,609	1,342,614	8,279,967
At vending machines, mobile vendors	388,754	31,833	38,236	83,360	269,021
At employer and school cafeterias	1,625,256	119,915	220,670	196,228	1,209,217
Restaurant and carry-out food on trips	**27,016,550**	**1,623,080**	**1,365,070**	**2,014,511**	**23,737,191**

* The category fast-food restaurants also includes take-out, delivery, concession stands, buffets, and cafeterias other than employer and school.
Note: "Asian" and "black" include Hispanics and non-Hispanics who identify themselves as being of the respective race alone. "Hispanic" includes people of any race who identify themselves as Hispanic. "Other" includes people who identify themselves as non-Hispanic and as Alaska Native, American Indian, Asian (who are also included in the "Asian" column), Native Hawaiian or other Pacific Islander, as well as non-Hispanics reporting more than one race. Numbers may not add to total because of rounding.
Source: Calculations by New Strategist based on the Bureau of Labor Statistics' 2010 Consumer Expenditure Survey

Table 23. Restaurants and Carry-Outs: Market shares by race and Hispanic origin, 2010

(percentage of total annual spending on restaurant and carry-out food accounted for by consumer unit race and Hispanic origin groups, 2010)

	total consumer units	Asian	black	Hispanic	non-Hispanic white and other
Share of total consumer units	100.0%	4.3%	12.2%	12.2%	75.8%
Share of total before-tax income	100.0	5.8	9.0	9.7	81.6
Share of total spending	100.0	5.2	9.1	10.5	80.6
RESTAURANTS AND CARRY-OUTS	100.0	6.1	8.6	12.1	79.6
Lunch	100.0	6.6	9.5	13.7	77.1
At fast-food restaurants*	100.0	6.9	11.0	15.6	73.7
At full-service restaurants	100.0	5.9	6.9	11.2	82.0
At vending machines, mobile vendors	100.0	3.5	8.8	19.8	71.9
At employer and school cafeterias	100.0	7.8	11.9	13.3	75.0
Dinner	100.0	6.1	8.3	11.2	80.7
At fast-food restaurants*	100.0	4.8	13.3	14.7	72.4
At full-service restaurants	100.0	6.7	5.7	9.4	84.9
At vending machines, mobile vendors	100.0	2.6	5.6	32.6	62.3
At employer and school cafeterias	100.0	10.8	5.5	8.2	86.2
Snacks and nonalcoholic beverages	100.0	5.4	8.7	13.0	78.5
At fast-food restaurants*	100.0	5.3	8.9	12.8	78.4
At full-service restaurants	100.0	3.9	8.0	12.4	79.8
At vending machines, mobile vendors	100.0	6.5	8.8	15.4	76.1
At employer and school cafeterias	100.0	11.6	6.6	11.8	81.6
Breakfast and brunch	100.0	4.6	10.5	14.4	75.5
At fast-food restaurants*	100.0	4.6	13.2	15.6	71.8
At full-service restaurants	100.0	3.9	6.6	13.1	80.6
At vending machines, mobile vendors	100.0	8.2	9.8	21.4	69.2
At employer and school cafeterias	100.0	7.4	13.6	12.1	74.4
Restaurant and carry-out food on trips	100.0	6.0	5.1	7.5	87.9

* The category fast-food restaurants also includes take-out, delivery, concession stands, buffets, and cafeterias other than employer and school.
Note: "Asian" and "black" include Hispanics and non-Hispanics who identify themselves as being of the respective race alone. "Hispanic" includes people of any race who identify themselves as Hispanic. "Other" includes people who identify themselves as non-Hispanic and as Alaska Native, American Indian, Asian (who are also included in the "Asian" column), Native Hawaiian or other Pacific Islander, as well as non-Hispanics reporting more than one race.
Source: Calculations by New Strategist based on the 2010 Consumer Expenditure Survey

Table 24. Restaurants and Carry-Outs: Average spending by region, 2010

(average annual spending of consumer units on restaurant and carry-out food, by region in which consumer unit lives, 2010)

	total consumer units	Northeast	Midwest	South	West
Number of consumer units (in 000s)	121,107	22,227	26,997	44,449	27,434
Number of persons per consumer unit	2.5	2.5	2.5	2.5	2.6
Average before-tax income of consumer units	$62,481.00	$68,409.00	$58,417.00	$58,824.00	$67,603.00
Average spending of consumer units, total	48,108.84	52,801.67	45,277.86	44,217.37	53,429.31
RESTAURANTS AND CARRY-OUTS	**2,304.02**	**2,604.05**	**1,969.09**	**2,151.65**	**2,647.23**
Lunch	**726.61**	**754.11**	**586.09**	**751.32**	**805.54**
At fast-food restaurants*	351.38	340.26	293.88	357.75	408.17
At full-service restaurants	285.15	303.85	205.27	305.71	316.77
At vending machines, mobile vendors	7.94	7.55	11.30	5.67	8.61
At employer and school cafeterias	82.14	102.45	75.63	82.19	71.99
Dinner	**986.99**	**1,156.86**	**831.52**	**904.51**	**1,140.91**
At fast-food restaurants*	331.42	323.86	316.27	329.72	355.77
At full-service restaurants	645.44	822.18	504.36	565.36	775.19
At vending machines, mobile vendors	2.86	1.85	3.51	2.65	3.37
At employer and school cafeterias	7.27	8.97	7.37	6.78	6.58
Snacks and nonalcoholic beverages	**155.29**	**188.65**	**138.86**	**130.82**	**184.90**
At fast-food restaurants*	102.25	115.40	90.86	85.56	130.47
At full-service restaurants	28.53	43.79	25.19	20.37	32.83
At vending machines, mobile vendors	18.59	21.77	18.44	18.77	15.85
At employer and school cafeterias	5.93	7.70	4.37	6.12	5.75
Breakfast and brunch	**212.05**	**261.80**	**187.83**	**178.63**	**250.85**
At fast-food restaurants*	110.61	143.05	86.71	100.11	125.50
At full-service restaurants	84.81	101.57	80.56	66.01	106.37
At vending machines, mobile vendors	3.21	4.22	3.29	2.46	3.56
At employer and school cafeterias	13.42	12.97	17.28	10.05	15.43
Restaurant and carry-out food on trips	**223.08**	**242.63**	**224.79**	**186.37**	**265.03**

* The category fast-food restaurants also includes take-out, delivery, concession stands, buffets, and cafeterias other than employer and school.
Source: Bureau of Labor Statistics, unpublished tables from the 2010 Consumer Expenditure Survey

Table 25. Restaurants and Carry-Outs: Indexed spending by region, 2010

(indexed average annual spending of consumer units on restaurant and carry-out food, by region in which consumer unit lives, 2010; index definition: an index of 100 is the average for all consumer units; an index of 125 means that spending by consumer units in that group is 25 percent above the average for all consumer units; an index of 75 indicates spending that is 25 percent below the average for all consumer units)

	total consumer units	Northeast	Midwest	South	West
Average spending of consumer units, total	$48,109	$52,802	$45,278	$44,217	$53,429
Average spending of consumer units, index	100	110	94	92	111
RESTAURANTS AND CARRY-OUTS	100	113	86	93	115
Lunch	100	104	81	103	111
At fast-food restaurants*	100	97	84	102	116
At full-service restaurants	100	107	72	107	111
At vending machines, mobile vendors	100	95	142	71	108
At employer and school cafeterias	100	125	92	100	88
Dinner	100	117	84	92	116
At fast-food restaurants*	100	98	95	100	107
At full-service restaurants	100	127	78	88	120
At vending machines, mobile vendors	100	65	123	93	118
At employer and school cafeterias	100	123	101	93	91
Snacks and nonalcoholic beverages	100	122	89	84	119
At fast-food restaurants*	100	113	89	84	128
At full-service restaurants	100	154	88	71	115
At vending machines, mobile vendors	100	117	99	101	85
At employer and school cafeterias	100	130	74	103	97
Breakfast and brunch	100	124	89	84	118
At fast-food restaurants*	100	129	78	91	114
At full-service restaurants	100	120	95	78	125
At vending machines, mobile vendors	100	132	103	77	111
At employer and school cafeterias	100	97	129	75	115
Restaurant and carry-out food on trips	100	109	101	84	119

* The category fast-food restaurants also includes take-out, delivery, concession stands, buffets, and cafeterias other than employer and school.
Source: Calculations by New Strategist based on the Bureau of Labor Statistics' 2010 Consumer Expenditure Survey

Table 26. Restaurants and Carry-Outs: Total spending by region, 2010

(total annual spending on restaurant and carry-out food, by region in which consumer unit lives, 2010; consumer units and dollars in thousands)

	total consumer units	Northeast	Midwest	South	West
Number of consumer units	121,107	22,227	26,997	44,449	27,434
Total spending of all consumer units	$5,826,317,286	$1,173,622,719	$1,222,366,386	$1,965,417,879	$1,465,779,691
RESTAURANTS AND CARRY-OUTS	279,032,950	57,880,219	53,159,523	95,638,691	72,624,108
Lunch	87,997,557	16,761,603	15,822,672	33,395,423	22,099,184
At fast-food restaurants*	42,554,578	7,562,959	7,933,878	15,901,630	11,197,736
At full-service restaurants	34,533,661	6,753,674	5,541,674	13,588,504	8,690,268
At vending machines, mobile vendors	961,590	167,814	305,066	252,026	236,207
At employer and school cafeterias	9,947,729	2,277,156	2,041,783	3,653,263	1,974,974
Dinner	119,531,398	25,713,527	22,448,545	40,204,565	31,299,725
At fast-food restaurants*	40,137,282	7,198,436	8,538,341	14,655,724	9,760,194
At full-service restaurants	78,167,302	18,274,595	13,616,207	25,129,687	21,266,563
At vending machines, mobile vendors	346,366	41,120	94,760	117,790	92,453
At employer and school cafeterias	880,448	199,376	198,968	301,364	180,516
Snacks and nonalcoholic beverages	18,806,706	4,193,124	3,748,803	5,814,818	5,072,547
At fast-food restaurants*	12,383,191	2,564,996	2,452,947	3,803,056	3,579,314
At full-service restaurants	3,455,183	973,320	680,054	905,426	900,658
At vending machines, mobile vendors	2,251,379	483,882	497,825	834,308	434,829
At employer and school cafeterias	718,165	171,148	117,977	272,028	157,746
Breakfast and brunch	25,680,739	5,819,029	5,070,847	7,939,925	6,881,819
At fast-food restaurants*	13,395,645	3,179,572	2,340,910	4,449,789	3,442,967
At full-service restaurants	10,271,085	2,257,596	2,174,878	2,934,079	2,918,155
At vending machines, mobile vendors	388,754	93,798	88,820	109,345	97,665
At employer and school cafeterias	1,625,256	288,284	466,508	446,713	423,307
Restaurant and carry-out food on trips	27,016,550	5,392,937	6,068,656	8,283,960	7,270,833

* The category fast-food restaurants also includes take-out, delivery, concession stands, buffets, and cafeterias other than employer and school.
Note: Numbers may not add to total because of rounding.
Source: Calculations by New Strategist based on the Bureau of Labor Statistics' 2010 Consumer Expenditure Survey

Table 27. Restaurants and Carry-Outs: Market shares by region, 2010

(percentage of total annual spending on restaurant and carry-out food accounted for by consumer units by region of residence, 2010)

	total consumer units	Northeast	Midwest	South	West
Share of total consumer units	100.0%	18.4%	22.3%	36.7%	22.7%
Share of total before-tax income	100.0	20.1	20.8	34.6	24.5
Share of total spending	100.0	20.1	21.0	33.7	25.2
RESTAURANTS AND CARRY-OUTS	100.0	20.7	19.1	34.3	26.0
Lunch	100.0	19.1	18.0	38.0	25.1
At fast-food restaurants*	100.0	17.8	18.6	37.4	26.3
At full-service restaurants	100.0	19.6	16.1	39.3	25.2
At vending machines, mobile vendors	100.0	17.5	31.7	26.2	24.6
At employer and school cafeterias	100.0	22.9	20.5	36.7	19.9
Dinner	100.0	21.5	18.8	33.6	26.2
At fast-food restaurants*	100.0	17.9	21.3	36.5	24.3
At full-service restaurants	100.0	23.4	17.4	32.1	27.2
At vending machines, mobile vendors	100.0	11.9	27.4	34.0	26.7
At employer and school cafeterias	100.0	22.6	22.6	34.2	20.5
Snacks and nonalcoholic beverages	100.0	22.3	19.9	30.9	27.0
At fast-food restaurants*	100.0	20.7	19.8	30.7	28.9
At full-service restaurants	100.0	28.2	19.7	26.2	26.1
At vending machines, mobile vendors	100.0	21.5	22.1	37.1	19.3
At employer and school cafeterias	100.0	23.8	16.4	37.9	22.0
Breakfast and brunch	100.0	22.7	19.7	30.9	26.8
At fast-food restaurants*	100.0	23.7	17.5	33.2	25.7
At full-service restaurants	100.0	22.0	21.2	28.6	28.4
At vending machines, mobile vendors	100.0	24.1	22.8	28.1	25.1
At employer and school cafeterias	100.0	17.7	28.7	27.5	26.1
Restaurant and carry-out food on trips	100.0	20.0	22.5	30.7	26.9

* The category fast-food restaurants also includes take-out, delivery, concession stands, buffets, and cafeterias other than employer and school.
Note: Numbers may not add to total because of rounding.
Source: Calculations by New Strategist based on the Bureau of Labor Statistics' 2010 Consumer Expenditure Survey

Table 28. Restaurants and Carry-Outs: Average spending by education, 2010

(average annual spending of consumer units on restaurant and carry-out food, by education of consumer unit reference person, 2010)

| | total consumer units | less than high school graduate | high school graduate | some college | associate's degree | bachelor's degree or more | | |
						total	bachelor's degree	master's, professional, doctorate
Number of consumer units (in 000s)	121,107	17,303	30,921	25,460	11,443	35,980	22,877	13,103
Number of persons per consumer unit	2.5	2.8	2.5	2.4	2.5	2.4	2.5	2.4
Average before-tax income of consumer units	$62,481.00	$33,317.00	$47,029.00	$52,113.00	$62,618.00	$97,080.00	$88,003.00	$112,927.00
Average spending of consumer units, total	48,108.84	29,753.22	37,968.62	43,143.68	50,967.27	68,189.19	63,906.84	75,751.61
RESTAURANTS AND CARRY-OUTS	**2,304.02**	**1,397.59**	**1,715.82**	**2,159.83**	**2,426.66**	**3,288.54**	**3,226.65**	**3,401.84**
Lunch	**726.61**	**489.22**	**574.23**	**689.46**	**780.49**	**974.46**	**968.73**	**985.74**
At fast-food restaurants*	351.38	279.89	297.29	361.07	387.71	411.27	411.70	410.42
At full-service restaurants	285.15	166.95	201.45	246.50	283.67	439.58	421.24	475.69
At vending machines, mobile vendors	7.94	6.93	8.85	6.33	6.25	9.32	10.43	7.14
At employer and school cafeterias	82.14	35.45	66.64	75.55	102.85	114.29	125.36	92.50
Dinner	**986.99**	**572.59**	**723.85**	**915.89**	**1,029.80**	**1,438.85**	**1,422.52**	**1,471.02**
At fast-food restaurants*	331.42	273.66	280.14	329.46	401.96	379.81	392.97	353.91
At full-service restaurants	645.44	291.56	434.37	571.59	619.73	1,049.74	1,020.62	1,107.10
At vending machines, mobile vendors	2.86	4.55	3.99	1.48	0.49	2.91	2.76	3.20
At employer and school cafeterias	7.27	2.82	5.34	13.36	7.61	6.38	6.16	6.82
Snacks and nonalcoholic beverages	**155.29**	**95.84**	**127.70**	**151.69**	**168.58**	**204.02**	**204.14**	**203.80**
At fast-food restaurants*	102.25	65.32	74.99	98.38	125.60	137.50	139.89	132.80
At full-service restaurants	28.53	11.20	29.08	23.52	22.42	41.41	39.68	44.81
At vending machines, mobile vendors	18.59	16.19	20.50	21.73	17.10	16.20	16.31	16.00
At employer and school cafeterias	5.93	3.13	3.12	8.06	3.46	8.91	8.26	10.18
Breakfast and brunch	**212.05**	**169.05**	**172.86**	**216.81**	**231.60**	**255.49**	**253.97**	**258.47**
At fast-food restaurants*	110.61	98.68	95.09	116.43	140.46	115.28	115.07	115.70
At full-service restaurants	84.81	58.28	65.96	85.05	76.78	115.63	118.51	109.95
At vending machines, mobile vendors	3.21	5.68	2.39	3.02	0.97	3.73	2.78	5.60
At employer and school cafeterias	13.42	6.41	9.42	12.31	13.38	20.84	17.61	27.21
Restaurant and carry-out food on trips	**223.08**	**70.89**	**117.18**	**185.98**	**216.19**	**415.72**	**377.29**	**482.81**

* The category fast-food restaurants also includes take-out, delivery, concession stands, buffets, and cafeterias other than employer and school.
Source: Bureau of Labor Statistics, unpublished tables from the 2010 Consumer Expenditure Survey

Table 29. Restaurants and Carry-Outs: Indexed spending by education, 2010

(indexed average annual spending of consumer units on restaurant and carry-out food, by education of consumer unit reference person, 2010; index definition: an index of 100 is the average for all consumer units; an index of 125 means that spending by consumer units in that group is 25 percent above the average for all consumer units; an index of 75 indicates spending that is 25 percent below the average for all consumer units)

	total consumer units	less than high school graduate	high school graduate	some college	associate's degree	bachelor's degree or more		
						total	bachelor's degree	master's, professional, doctorate
Average spending of consumer units, total	$48,109	$29,753	$37,969	$43,144	$50,967	$68,189	$63,907	$75,752
Average spending of consumer units, index	100	62	79	90	106	142	133	158
RESTAURANTS AND CARRY-OUTS	**100**	**61**	**75**	**94**	**105**	**143**	**140**	**148**
Lunch	**100**	**67**	**79**	**95**	**107**	**134**	**133**	**136**
At fast-food restaurants*	100	80	85	103	110	117	117	117
At full-service restaurants	100	59	71	86	100	154	148	167
At vending machines, mobile vendors	100	87	112	80	79	117	131	90
At employer and school cafeterias	100	43	81	92	125	139	153	113
Dinner	**100**	**58**	**73**	**93**	**104**	**146**	**144**	**149**
At fast-food restaurants*	100	83	85	99	121	115	119	107
At full-service restaurants	100	45	67	89	96	163	158	172
At vending machines, mobile vendors	100	159	140	52	17	102	97	112
At employer and school cafeterias	100	39	74	184	105	88	85	94
Snacks and nonalcoholic beverages	**100**	**62**	**82**	**98**	**109**	**131**	**132**	**131**
At fast-food restaurants*	100	64	73	96	123	135	137	130
At full-service restaurants	100	39	102	82	79	145	139	157
At vending machines, mobile vendors	100	87	110	117	92	87	88	86
At employer and school cafeterias	100	53	53	136	58	150	139	172
Breakfast and brunch	**100**	**80**	**82**	**102**	**109**	**121**	**120**	**122**
At fast-food restaurants*	100	89	86	105	127	104	104	105
At full-service restaurants	100	69	78	100	91	136	140	130
At vending machines, mobile vendors	100	177	75	94	30	116	87	175
At employer and school cafeterias	100	48	70	92	100	155	131	203
Restaurant and carry-out food on trips	**100**	**32**	**53**	**83**	**97**	**186**	**169**	**216**

* The category fast-food restaurants also includes take-out, delivery, concession stands, buffets, and cafeterias other than employer and school.
Source: Calculations by New Strategist based on the Bureau of Labor Statistics' 2010 Consumer Expenditure Survey

Table 30. Restaurants and Carry-Outs: Total spending by education, 2010

(total annual spending on restaurant and carry-out food, by education of consumer unit reference person, 2010; consumer units and dollars in thousands)

	total consumer units	less than high school graduate	high school graduate	some college	associate's degree	bachelor's degree or more		
						total	bachelor's degree	master's, professional, doctorate
Number of consumer units	121,107	17,303	30,921	25,460	11,443	35,980	22,877	13,103
Total spending of all consumer units	$5,826,317,286	$514,819,966	$1,174,027,699	$1,098,438,093	$583,218,471	$2,453,447,056	$1,461,996,779	$992,573,346
RESTAURANTS AND CARRY-OUTS	279,032,950	24,182,500	53,054,870	54,989,272	27,768,270	118,321,669	73,816,072	44,574,310
Lunch	87,997,557	8,464,974	17,755,766	17,553,652	8,931,147	35,061,071	22,161,636	12,916,151
At fast-food restaurants*	42,554,578	4,842,937	9,192,504	9,192,842	4,436,566	14,797,495	9,418,461	5,377,733
At full-service restaurants	34,533,661	2,888,736	6,229,035	6,275,890	3,246,036	15,816,088	9,636,708	6,232,966
At vending machines, mobile vendors	961,590	119,910	273,651	161,162	71,519	335,334	238,607	93,555
At employer and school cafeterias	9,947,729	613,391	2,060,575	1,923,503	1,176,913	4,112,154	2,867,861	1,212,028
Dinner	119,531,398	9,907,525	22,382,166	23,318,559	11,784,001	51,769,823	32,542,990	19,274,775
At fast-food restaurants*	40,137,282	4,735,139	8,662,209	8,388,052	4,599,628	13,665,564	8,989,975	4,637,283
At full-service restaurants	78,167,302	5,044,863	13,431,155	14,552,681	7,091,570	37,769,645	23,348,724	14,506,331
At vending machines, mobile vendors	346,366	78,729	123,375	37,681	5,607	104,702	63,141	41,930
At employer and school cafeterias	880,448	48,795	165,118	340,146	87,081	229,552	140,922	89,363
Snacks and nonalcoholic beverages	18,806,706	1,658,320	3,948,612	3,862,027	1,929,061	7,340,640	4,670,111	2,670,391
At fast-food restaurants*	12,383,191	1,130,232	2,318,766	2,504,755	1,437,241	4,947,250	3,200,264	1,740,078
At full-service restaurants	3,455,183	193,794	899,183	598,819	256,552	1,489,932	907,759	587,145
At vending machines, mobile vendors	2,251,379	280,136	633,881	553,246	195,675	582,876	373,124	209,648
At employer and school cafeterias	718,165	54,158	96,474	205,208	39,593	320,582	188,964	133,389
Breakfast and brunch	25,680,739	2,925,072	5,345,004	5,519,983	2,650,199	9,192,530	5,810,072	3,386,732
At fast-food restaurants*	13,395,645	1,707,460	2,940,278	2,964,308	1,607,284	4,147,774	2,632,456	1,516,017
At full-service restaurants	10,271,085	1,008,419	2,039,549	2,165,373	878,594	4,160,367	2,711,153	1,440,675
At vending machines, mobile vendors	388,754	98,281	73,901	76,889	11,100	134,205	63,598	73,377
At employer and school cafeterias	1,625,256	110,912	291,276	313,413	153,107	749,823	402,864	356,533
Restaurant and carry-out food on trips	27,016,550	1,226,610	3,623,323	4,735,051	2,473,862	14,957,606	8,631,263	6,326,259

* The category fast-food restaurants also includes take-out, delivery, concession stands, buffets, and cafeterias other than employer and school.

Note: Numbers may not add to total because of rounding.

Source: Calculations by New Strategist based on the Bureau of Labor Statistics' 2010 Consumer Expenditure Survey

Table 31. Restaurants and Carry-Outs: Market shares by education, 2010

(percentage of total annual spending on restaurant and carry-out food accounted for by education of consumer unit reference person, 2010)

	total consumer units	less than high school graduate	high school graduate	some college	associate's degree	bachelor's degree or more total	bachelor's degree	master's, professional, doctorate
Share of total consumer units	100.0%	14.3%	25.5%	21.0%	9.4%	29.7%	18.9%	10.8%
Share of total before-tax income	100.0	7.6	19.2	17.5	9.5	46.2	26.6	19.6
Share of total spending	100.0	8.8	20.2	18.9	10.0	42.1	25.1	17.0
RESTAURANTS AND CARRY-OUTS	**100.0**	**8.7**	**19.0**	**19.7**	**10.0**	**42.4**	**26.5**	**16.0**
Lunch	**100.0**	**9.6**	**20.2**	**19.9**	**10.1**	**39.8**	**25.2**	**14.7**
At fast-food restaurants*	100.0	11.4	21.6	21.6	10.4	34.8	22.1	12.6
At full-service restaurants	100.0	8.4	18.0	18.2	9.4	45.8	27.9	18.1
At vending machines, mobile vendors	100.0	12.5	28.5	16.8	7.4	34.9	24.8	9.7
At employer and school cafeterias	100.0	6.2	20.7	19.3	11.8	41.3	28.8	12.2
Dinner	**100.0**	**8.3**	**18.7**	**19.5**	**9.9**	**43.3**	**27.2**	**16.1**
At fast-food restaurants*	100.0	11.8	21.6	20.9	11.5	34.1	22.4	11.6
At full-service restaurants	100.0	6.5	17.2	18.6	9.1	48.3	29.9	18.6
At vending machines, mobile vendors	100.0	22.7	35.6	10.9	1.6	30.2	18.2	12.1
At employer and school cafeterias	100.0	5.5	18.8	38.6	9.9	26.1	16.0	10.1
Snacks and nonalcoholic beverages	**100.0**	**8.8**	**21.0**	**20.5**	**10.3**	**39.0**	**24.8**	**14.2**
At fast-food restaurants*	100.0	9.1	18.7	20.2	11.6	40.0	25.8	14.1
At full-service restaurants	100.0	5.6	26.0	17.3	7.4	43.1	26.3	17.0
At vending machines, mobile vendors	100.0	12.4	28.2	24.6	8.7	25.9	16.6	9.3
At employer and school cafeterias	100.0	7.5	13.4	28.6	5.5	44.6	26.3	18.6
Breakfast and brunch	**100.0**	**11.4**	**20.8**	**21.5**	**10.3**	**35.8**	**22.6**	**13.2**
At fast-food restaurants*	100.0	12.7	21.9	22.1	12.0	31.0	19.7	11.3
At full-service restaurants	100.0	9.8	19.9	21.1	8.6	40.5	26.4	14.0
At vending machines, mobile vendors	100.0	25.3	19.0	19.8	2.9	34.5	16.4	18.9
At employer and school cafeterias	100.0	6.8	17.9	19.3	9.4	46.1	24.8	21.9
Restaurant and carry-out food on trips	**100.0**	**4.5**	**13.4**	**17.5**	**9.2**	**55.4**	**31.9**	**23.4**

* The category fast-food restaurants also includes take-out, delivery, concession stands, buffets, and cafeterias other than employer and school.
Note: Numbers may not add to total because of rounding.
Source: Calculations by New Strategist based on the Bureau of Labor Statistics' 2010 Consumer Expenditure Survey

Breakfast and Brunch at Fast-Food Restaurants, Including Take-Outs, Deliveries, Concession Stands, Buffets, and Cafeterias (except Employer and School)

Best customers: Householders aged 25 to 44
                      Married couples with school-aged or older children at home
                      Hispanics, Asians, and blacks
                      Households in the Northeast

Customer trends: Average household spending on breakfast at fast-food restaurants is
                       likely to stabilize as the large millennial generation fills the best-customer
                       age group.

The busiest people are the biggest spenders on breakfast at fast-food restaurants—workers and parents. Householders of prime working age, 25 to 44, spend 23 to 33 percent more than average on this item. Married couples with school-aged or older children at home spend 23 to 33 percent more than average on breakfast at fast-food restaurants as they try to fit meals into their busy schedules. Hispanics spend 28 percent more than average on breakfast at fast-food restaurants, and Asians and blacks spend 8 percent more. Together the three minority groups control one-third of the market. Households in the Northeast outspend the average by 29 percent.

Breakfast at fast-food restaurants is the category in this report that suffered the smallest decline in spending between 2006 and 2010, a 5 percent drop after adjusting for inflation. Spending on this item is likely to stabilize as the large millennial generation fills the best-customer age group.

Table 32. Breakfast and brunch at fast-food restaurants, including take-outs, deliveries, concession stands, buffets, and cafeterias (except employer and school)

Total household spending $13,395,645,270.00
Average household spends   110.61

	AVERAGE HOUSEHOLD SPENDING	BEST CUSTOMERS (index)	BIGGEST CUSTOMERS (market share)
AGE OF HOUSEHOLDER			
Average household	**$110.61**	**100**	**100.0%**
Under age 25	78.54	71	4.7
Aged 25 to 34	147.30	133	22.2
Aged 35 to 44	135.76	123	22.2
Aged 45 to 54	125.16	113	23.4
Aged 55 to 64	94.42	85	15.1
Aged 65 to 74	90.36	82	8.8
Aged 75 or older	42.16	38	3.6

	AVERAGE HOUSEHOLD SPENDING	BEST CUSTOMERS (index)	BIGGEST CUSTOMERS (market share)
HOUSEHOLD INCOME			
Average household	**$110.61**	**100**	**100.0%**
Under $20,000	61.97	56	12.2
$20,000 to $39,999	85.62	77	17.7
$40,000 to $49,999	112.10	101	9.6
$50,000 to $69,999	114.92	104	14.9
$70,000 to $79,999	133.19	120	7.2
$80,000 to $99,999	146.39	132	11.0
$100,000 or more	177.29	160	27.5
HOUSEHOLD TYPE			
Average household	**110.61**	**100**	**100.0**
Married couples	121.92	110	54.4
Married couples, no children	99.91	90	19.2
Married couples, with children	138.08	125	29.0
Oldest child under age 6	116.48	105	4.5
Oldest child aged 6 to 17	147.02	133	15.6
Oldest child aged 18 or older	135.80	123	8.9
Single parent with child under age 18	96.76	87	5.2
Single person	84.15	76	22.3
RACE AND HISPANIC ORIGIN			
Average household	**110.61**	**100**	**100.0**
Asian	119.81	108	4.6
Black	119.19	108	13.2
Hispanic	141.42	128	15.6
Non-Hispanic white and other	104.77	95	71.8
REGION			
Average household	**110.61**	**100**	**100.0**
Northeast	143.05	129	23.7
Midwest	86.71	78	17.5
South	100.11	91	33.2
West	125.50	113	25.7
EDUCATION			
Average household	**110.61**	**100**	**100.0**
Less than high school graduate	98.68	89	12.7
High school graduate	95.09	86	21.9
Some college	116.43	105	22.1
Associate's degree	140.46	127	12.0
Bachelor's degree or more	115.28	104	31.0
Bachelor's degree	115.07	104	19.7
Master's, professional, doctoral degree	115.70	105	11.3

Note: Market shares may not sum to 100.0 because of rounding and missing categories by household type. "Asian" and "black" include Hispanics and non-Hispanics who identify themselves as being of the respective race alone. "Hispanic" includes people of any race who identify themselves as Hispanic. "Other" includes people who identify themselves as non-Hispanic and as Alaska Native, American Indian, Asian (who are also included in the "Asian" row), Native Hawaiian or other Pacific Islander, as well as non-Hispanics reporting more than one race.
Source: Calculations by New Strategist based on the Bureau of Labor Statistics' 2010 Consumer Expenditure Survey

Breakfast and Brunch at Full-Service Restaurants

Best customers:
    Householders aged 65 to 74
    Married couples without children at home
    Households in the Northeast and West

Customer trends:
    Average household spending on breakfast at full-service restaurants may rise as baby boomers fill the best-customer age group—but only if discretionary income grows.

The biggest spenders on breakfast and brunch at full-service restaurants are older married couples enjoying a leisurely meal. Householders aged 65 to 74 spend 18 percent more than average on this item. Married couples without children at home (many of them empty-nesters) spend 32 percent more than average on breakfast and brunch at full-service restaurants. Households in the Northeast and West spend, respectively, 20 and 25 percent more than average on breakfast and brunch at full-service restaurants.

Average household spending on breakfast at full-service restaurants declined by a substantial 29 percent between 2006 and 2010, after adjusting for inflation. Behind the decline was the Great Recession and a reduction in spending on all types of restaurant meals. In the years ahead, spending on full-service breakfasts should rise as boomers fill the best-customer age group—but only if discretionary income grows.

Table 33. Breakfast and brunch at full-service restaurants

Total household spending	$10,271,084,670.00
Average household spends	84.81

	AVERAGE HOUSEHOLD SPENDING	BEST CUSTOMERS (index)	BIGGEST CUSTOMERS (market share)
AGE OF HOUSEHOLDER			
Average household	**$84.81**	**100**	**100.0%**
Under age 25	57.30	68	4.5
Aged 25 to 34	79.52	94	15.6
Aged 35 to 44	86.66	102	18.5
Aged 45 to 54	87.42	103	21.3
Aged 55 to 64	85.26	101	17.7
Aged 65 to 74	100.00	118	12.7
Aged 75 or older	85.96	101	9.7

	AVERAGE HOUSEHOLD SPENDING	BEST CUSTOMERS (index)	BIGGEST CUSTOMERS (market share)
HOUSEHOLD INCOME			
Average household	**$84.81**	**100**	**100.0%**
Under $20,000	35.14	41	9.0
$20,000 to $39,999	56.83	67	15.4
$40,000 to $49,999	81.96	97	9.1
$50,000 to $69,999	105.51	124	17.8
$70,000 to $79,999	104.12	123	7.3
$80,000 to $99,999	116.98	138	11.5
$100,000 or more	147.81	174	29.9
HOUSEHOLD TYPE			
Average household	**84.81**	**100**	**100.0**
Married couples	101.26	119	58.9
Married couples, no children	111.80	132	28.0
Married couples, with children	84.69	100	23.2
Oldest child under age 6	46.29	55	2.3
Oldest child aged 6 to 17	99.03	117	13.7
Oldest child aged 18 or older	82.95	98	7.1
Single parent with child under age 18	38.49	45	2.7
Single person	65.99	78	22.8
RACE AND HISPANIC ORIGIN			
Average household	**84.81**	**100**	**100.0**
Asian	78.18	92	3.9
Black	46.06	54	6.6
Hispanic	91.00	107	13.1
Non-Hispanic white and other	90.18	106	80.6
REGION			
Average household	**84.81**	**100**	**100.0**
Northeast	101.57	120	22.0
Midwest	80.56	95	21.2
South	66.01	78	28.6
West	106.37	125	28.4
EDUCATION			
Average household	**84.81**	**100**	**100.0**
Less than high school graduate	58.28	69	9.8
High school graduate	65.96	78	19.9
Some college	85.05	100	21.1
Associate's degree	76.78	91	8.6
Bachelor's degree or more	115.63	136	40.5
Bachelor's degree	118.51	140	26.4
Master's, professional, doctoral degree	109.95	130	14.0

Note: Market shares may not sum to 100.0 because of rounding and missing categories by household type. "Asian" and "black" include Hispanics and non-Hispanics who identify themselves as being of the respective race alone. "Hispanic" includes people of any race who identify themselves as Hispanic. "Other" includes people who identify themselves as non-Hispanic and as Alaska Native, American Indian, Asian (who are also included in the "Asian" row), Native Hawaiian or other Pacific Islander, as well as non-Hispanics reporting more than one race.
Source: Calculations by New Strategist based on the Bureau of Labor Statistics' 2010 Consumer Expenditure Survey

Dinner at Fast-Food Restaurants, Including Take-Outs, Deliveries, Concession Stands, Buffets, and Cafeterias (except Employer and School)

Best customers: Householders aged 25 to 44
Married couples with children at home
Single parents
Hispanics, Asians, and blacks

Customer trends: Average household spending on dinner at fast-food restaurants may grow because the large millennial generation is moving into the best-customer lifestage.

Families with children are the biggest spenders on dinners at fast-food restaurants. Householders ranging in age from 25 to 44 spend 27 to 51 percent more than average on this item and account for 48 percent of the market. Married couples with children at home spend 54 percent more than average on dinner at fast-food restaurants as they try to fit meals into their busy schedules. Single parents, whose spending approaches average on only a few items, spend 15 percent more than average on fast-food dinners. Blacks, Asians, and Hispanics spend between 9 and 20 percent more than average on fast-food dinners and together account for nearly one-third of the market.

Average household spending on dinner at fast-food restaurants fell 9 percent between 2006 and 2010 as households cut their spending during the economic downturn. Because the large millennial generation is moving into the best-customer lifestage, average household spending on fast-food restaurant dinners may grow in the years ahead.

Table 34. Dinner at fast-food restaurants, including take-outs, deliveries, concession stands, buffets, and cafeterias (except employer and school)

Total household spending $40,137,281,940.00
Average household spends   331.42

	AVERAGE HOUSEHOLD SPENDING	BEST CUSTOMERS (index)	BIGGEST CUSTOMERS (market share)
AGE OF HOUSEHOLDER			
Average household	**$331.42**	**100**	**100.0%**
Under age 25	332.68	100	6.7
Aged 25 to 34	421.32	127	21.2
Aged 35 to 44	499.01	151	27.2
Aged 45 to 54	368.08	111	23.0
Aged 55 to 64	263.55	80	14.0
Aged 65 to 74	158.40	48	5.1
Aged 75 or older	100.14	30	2.9

	AVERAGE HOUSEHOLD SPENDING	BEST CUSTOMERS (index)	BIGGEST CUSTOMERS (market share)
HOUSEHOLD INCOME			
Average household	**$331.42**	**100**	**100.0%**
Under $20,000	175.02	53	11.5
$20,000 to $39,999	231.57	70	16.0
$40,000 to $49,999	344.92	104	9.8
$50,000 to $69,999	372.31	112	16.1
$70,000 to $79,999	412.55	124	7.5
$80,000 to $99,999	429.80	130	10.8
$100,000 or more	550.08	166	28.5
HOUSEHOLD TYPE			
Average household	**331.42**	**100**	**100.0**
Married couples	403.38	122	60.0
Married couples, no children	269.44	81	17.3
Married couples, with children	509.83	154	35.8
Oldest child under age 6	450.83	136	5.8
Oldest child aged 6 to 17	541.20	163	19.2
Oldest child aged 18 or older	493.24	149	10.7
Single parent with child under age 18	382.03	115	6.8
Single person	180.10	54	15.9
RACE AND HISPANIC ORIGIN			
Average household	**331.42**	**100**	**100.0**
Asian	373.80	113	4.8
Black	361.28	109	13.3
Hispanic	399.30	120	14.7
Non-Hispanic white and other	316.34	95	72.4
REGION			
Average household	**331.42**	**100**	**100.0**
Northeast	323.86	98	17.9
Midwest	316.27	95	21.3
South	329.72	99	36.5
West	355.77	107	24.3
EDUCATION			
Average household	**331.42**	**100**	**100.0**
Less than high school graduate	273.66	83	11.8
High school graduate	280.14	85	21.6
Some college	329.46	99	20.9
Associate's degree	401.96	121	11.5
Bachelor's degree or more	379.81	115	34.0
Bachelor's degree	392.97	119	22.4
Master's, professional, doctoral degree	353.91	107	11.6

Note: Market shares may not sum to 100.0 because of rounding and missing categories by household type. "Asian" and "black" include Hispanics and non-Hispanics who identify themselves as being of the respective race alone. "Hispanic" includes people of any race who identify themselves as Hispanic. "Other" includes people who identify themselves as non-Hispanic and as Alaska Native, American Indian, Asian (who are also included in the "Asian" row), Native Hawaiian or other Pacific Islander, as well as non-Hispanics reporting more than one race.
Source: Calculations by New Strategist based on the Bureau of Labor Statistics' 2010 Consumer Expenditure Survey

Dinner at Full-Service Restaurants

Best customers: Householders aged 25 to 54
Married couples without children at home
Married couples with school-aged or older children at home
Asians
Households in the Northeast and West

Customer trends: Average household spending on dinner at full-service restaurants should rise in the years ahead as growing numbers of baby boomers retire and gain more free time—but only if discretionary income grows.

The biggest spenders on dinners at full-service restaurants are married couples with children as well as empty-nesters. Householders ranging in age from 25 to 54 spend 8 to 26 percent more than average on this item. Married couples with school-aged children spend 40 percent, and those with adult children at home, 27 percent more than average on this item. Married couples without children at home (many of them empty-nesters) spend 23 percent more than average on full-service restaurant dinners. Asians spend 58 percent more than average on full-service dinners. Households in the Northeast lead those in other regions in full-service dinner spending—their bill is 27 percent higher than average. In the West, households spend 20 percent more.

Average household spending on dinners in full-service restaurants fell by 18 percent between 2006 and 2010, after adjusting for inflation, as households cut their budgets in the midst of the economic downturn. Spending in the category should rise in the years ahead as baby boomers retire and gain more free time—but only if discretionary income grows.

Table 35. Dinner at full-service restaurants

Total household spending $78,167,302,080.00
Average household spends   645.44

	AVERAGE HOUSEHOLD SPENDING	BEST CUSTOMERS (index)	BIGGEST CUSTOMERS (market share)
AGE OF HOUSEHOLDER			
Average household	**$645.44**	**100**	**100.0%**
Under age 25	372.23	58	3.8
Aged 25 to 34	698.48	108	18.0
Aged 35 to 44	811.09	126	22.7
Aged 45 to 54	713.77	111	22.9
Aged 55 to 64	648.73	101	17.7
Aged 65 to 74	573.81	89	9.6
Aged 75 or older	355.07	55	5.2

	AVERAGE HOUSEHOLD SPENDING	BEST CUSTOMERS (index)	BIGGEST CUSTOMERS (market share)
HOUSEHOLD INCOME			
Average household	**$645.44**	**100**	**100.0%**
Under $20,000	208.42	32	7.0
$20,000 to $39,999	349.73	54	12.4
$40,000 to $49,999	514.37	80	7.5
$50,000 to $69,999	653.92	101	14.5
$70,000 to $79,999	835.13	129	7.7
$80,000 to $99,999	859.48	133	11.1
$100,000 or more	1,525.93	236	40.5
HOUSEHOLD TYPE			
Average household	**645.44**	**100**	**100.0**
Married couples	809.63	125	61.9
Married couples, no children	792.26	123	26.1
Married couples, with children	854.08	132	30.8
Oldest child under age 6	764.46	118	5.1
Oldest child aged 6 to 17	906.44	140	16.5
Oldest child aged 18 or older	821.89	127	9.2
Single parent with child under age 18	323.55	50	3.0
Single person	452.71	70	20.5
RACE AND HISPANIC ORIGIN			
Average household	**645.44**	**100**	**100.0**
Asian	1,022.51	158	6.7
Black	301.50	47	5.7
Hispanic	498.66	77	9.4
Non-Hispanic white and other	723.02	112	84.9
REGION			
Average household	**645.44**	**100**	**100.0**
Northeast	822.18	127	23.4
Midwest	504.36	78	17.4
South	565.36	88	32.1
West	775.19	120	27.2
EDUCATION			
Average household	**645.44**	**100**	**100.0**
Less than high school graduate	291.56	45	6.5
High school graduate	434.37	67	17.2
Some college	571.59	89	18.6
Associate's degree	619.73	96	9.1
Bachelor's degree or more	1,049.74	163	48.3
Bachelor's degree	1,020.62	158	29.9
Master's, professional, doctoral degree	1,107.10	172	18.6

Note: Market shares may not sum to 100.0 because of rounding and missing categories by household type. "Asian" and "black" include Hispanics and non-Hispanics who identify themselves as being of the respective race alone. "Hispanic" includes people of any race who identify themselves as Hispanic. "Other" includes people who identify themselves as non-Hispanic and as Alaska Native, American Indian, Asian (who are also included in the "Asian" row), Native Hawaiian or other Pacific Islander, as well as non-Hispanics reporting more than one race.
Source: Calculations by New Strategist based on the Bureau of Labor Statistics' 2010 Consumer Expenditure Survey

Lunch at Employer and School Cafeterias

Best customers: Householders aged 35 to 54
                       Married couples with school-aged or older children at home
                       Single parents
                       Asians
                       Households in the Northeast

Customer trends: Average household spending on lunch at employer and school cafeterias
                       may continue to decline as more children qualify for subsidized lunches and
                       fewer employers offer cafeteria meals in an attempt to cut costs.

Not surprisingly, parents and workers are the biggest spenders on lunch at employer and school cafeterias. Householders aged 35 to 54, most of them in the workforce, spend 44 to 101 percent more than average on this item and account for two-thirds of the market. Married couples with school-aged children, many of them dual-income couples, spend two-and-one-half times the average on this item. Couples with adult children at home spend nearly twice the average on employer and school cafeteria lunches, while single parents spend over twice the average. Asians also spend nearly double the average on this item. The spending on lunch at employer and school cafeterias of Northeastern householders is one-quarter higher than average.

Average household spending on lunch at employer and school cafeterias fell 12 percent between 2006 and 2010, after adjusting for inflation. Behind the decline was household budget cutting in the midst of the economic downturn. This category may continue to decline as a growing percentage of children qualify for subsidized lunches and fewer employers offer cafeteria meals in an attempt to cut costs.

Table 36. Lunch at employer and school cafeterias

Total household spending $9,947,728,980.00
Average household spends   82.14

	AVERAGE HOUSEHOLD SPENDING	BEST CUSTOMERS (index)	BIGGEST CUSTOMERS (market share)
AGE OF HOUSEHOLDER			
Average household	**$82.14**	**100**	**100.0%**
Under age 25	86.47	105	7.0
Aged 25 to 34	73.29	89	14.9
Aged 35 to 44	165.44	201	36.4
Aged 45 to 54	118.12	144	29.7
Aged 55 to 64	38.13	46	8.2
Aged 65 to 74	19.83	24	2.6
Aged 75 or older	11.16	14	1.3

	AVERAGE HOUSEHOLD SPENDING	BEST CUSTOMERS (index)	BIGGEST CUSTOMERS (market share)
HOUSEHOLD INCOME			
Average household	**$82.14**	**100**	**100.0%**
Under $20,000	30.65	37	8.1
$20,000 to $39,999	51.47	63	14.4
$40,000 to $49,999	58.14	71	6.7
$50,000 to $69,999	106.73	130	18.6
$70,000 to $79,999	61.21	75	4.5
$80,000 to $99,999	122.00	149	12.4
$100,000 or more	172.79	210	36.1
HOUSEHOLD TYPE			
Average household	**82.14**	**100**	**100.0**
Married couples	102.94	125	61.8
Married couples, no children	30.87	38	8.0
Married couples, with children	166.18	202	47.1
Oldest child under age 6	55.57	68	2.9
Oldest child aged 6 to 17	208.71	254	29.9
Oldest child aged 18 or older	159.38	194	14.0
Single parent with child under age 18	171.11	208	12.3
Single person	31.99	39	11.4
RACE AND HISPANIC ORIGIN			
Average household	**82.14**	**100**	**100.0**
Asian	150.87	184	7.8
Black	79.88	97	11.9
Hispanic	89.89	109	13.3
Non-Hispanic white and other	81.24	99	75.0
REGION			
Average household	**82.14**	**100**	**100.0**
Northeast	102.45	125	22.9
Midwest	75.63	92	20.5
South	82.19	100	36.7
West	71.99	88	19.9
EDUCATION			
Average household	**82.14**	**100**	**100.0**
Less than high school graduate	35.45	43	6.2
High school graduate	66.64	81	20.7
Some college	75.55	92	19.3
Associate's degree	102.85	125	11.8
Bachelor's degree or more	114.29	139	41.3
Bachelor's degree	125.36	153	28.8
Master's, professional, doctoral degree	92.50	113	12.2

Note: Market shares may not sum to 100.0 because of rounding and missing categories by household type. "Asian" and "black" include Hispanics and non-Hispanics who identify themselves as being of the respective race alone. "Hispanic" includes people of any race who identify themselves as Hispanic. "Other" includes people who identify themselves as non-Hispanic and as Alaska Native, American Indian, Asian (who are also included in the "Asian" row), Native Hawaiian or other Pacific Islander, as well as non-Hispanics reporting more than one race.
Source: Calculations by New Strategist based on the Bureau of Labor Statistics' 2010 Consumer Expenditure Survey

Lunch at Fast-Food Restaurants, Including Take-Outs, Deliveries, Concession Stands, Buffets, and Cafeterias (except Employer and School)

Best customers: Householders aged 25 to 44
Married couples with children at home
Asians and Hispanics

Customer trends: Average household spending on lunch at fast-food restaurants may continue to decline as boomers begin to retire and have time for more leisurely lunches at full-service restaurants.

Workers and parents are the best customers of fast-food lunches. Householders of prime working age, 25 to 44, spend 27 to 34 percent more than average on this item and account for 45 percent of the market. Married couples with children at home spend 41 percent more than average on lunches at fast-food restaurants as they try to fit meals into their busy schedules. Asians spend 62 percent more than average on this item, and Hispanics, 28 percent.

Average household spending on fast-food lunches fell by 12 percent between 2006 and 2010, after adjusting for inflation. Behind the decline was belt-tightening as households cut their budget in the midst of the economic downturn. Spending on this item may continue to decline in the years ahead as boomers begin to retire.

Table 37. Lunch at fast-food restaurants, including take-outs, deliveries, concession stands, buffets, and cafeterias (except employer and school)

Total household spending $42,554,577,660.00
Average household spends 351.38

AGE OF HOUSEHOLDER	AVERAGE HOUSEHOLD SPENDING	BEST CUSTOMERS (index)	BIGGEST CUSTOMERS (market share)
Average household	$351.38	100	100.0%
Under age 25	309.91	88	5.9
Aged 25 to 34	445.15	127	21.1
Aged 35 to 44	470.00	134	24.2
Aged 45 to 54	379.18	108	22.3
Aged 55 to 64	324.47	92	16.3
Aged 65 to 74	219.81	63	6.7
Aged 75 or older	130.90	37	3.6

	AVERAGE HOUSEHOLD SPENDING	BEST CUSTOMERS (index)	BIGGEST CUSTOMERS (market share)
HOUSEHOLD INCOME			
Average household	**$351.38**	**100**	**100.0%**
Under $20,000	188.32	54	11.7
$20,000 to $39,999	246.94	70	16.1
$40,000 to $49,999	346.74	99	9.3
$50,000 to $69,999	377.68	107	15.4
$70,000 to $79,999	445.83	127	7.6
$80,000 to $99,999	469.75	134	11.1
$100,000 or more	592.26	169	28.9
HOUSEHOLD TYPE			
Average household	**351.38**	**100**	**100.0**
Married couples	412.42	117	57.9
Married couples, no children	298.52	85	18.0
Married couples, with children	495.50	141	32.8
Oldest child under age 6	436.52	124	5.3
Oldest child aged 6 to 17	495.48	141	16.6
Oldest child aged 18 or older	525.72	150	10.8
Single parent with child under age 18	326.54	93	5.5
Single person	224.42	64	18.7
RACE AND HISPANIC ORIGIN			
Average household	**351.38**	**100**	**100.0**
Asian	569.22	162	6.9
Black	315.08	90	11.0
Hispanic	449.39	128	15.6
Non-Hispanic white and other	341.56	97	73.7
REGION			
Average household	**351.38**	**100**	**100.0**
Northeast	340.26	97	17.8
Midwest	293.88	84	18.6
South	357.75	102	37.4
West	408.17	116	26.3
EDUCATION			
Average household	**351.38**	**100**	**100.0**
Less than high school graduate	279.89	80	11.4
High school graduate	297.29	85	21.6
Some college	361.07	103	21.6
Associate's degree	387.71	110	10.4
Bachelor's degree or more	411.27	117	34.8
Bachelor's degree	411.70	117	22.1
Master's, professional, doctoral degree	410.42	117	12.6

Note: Market shares may not sum to 100.0 because of rounding and missing categories by household type. "Asian" and "black" include Hispanics and non-Hispanics who identify themselves as being of the respective race alone. "Hispanic" includes people of any race who identify themselves as Hispanic. "Other" includes people who identify themselves as non-Hispanic and as Alaska Native, American Indian, Asian (who are also included in the "Asian" row), Native Hawaiian or other Pacific Islander, as well as non-Hispanics reporting more than one race.
Source: Calculations by New Strategist based on the Bureau of Labor Statistics' 2010 Consumer Expenditure Survey

Lunch at Full-Service Restaurants

Best customers: Householders aged 65 to 74
Married couples
Asians

Customer trends: Average household spending on lunch at full-service restaurants should rise as growing numbers of baby boomers become empty-nesters with more free time—but only if discretionary income grows.

The biggest spenders on lunch at full-service restaurants are older married couples enjoying a leisurely meal. Householders aged 65 to 74 spend 20 percent more than average on this item. Married couples without children at home (many of them empty-nesters) spend 37 percent more than average on lunch at full-service restaurants. Couples with children at home spend one-quarter more than average on full-service lunches, in part because their households are larger than average. Asians outspend the average on lunch at full-service restaurants by 38 percent.

Average household spending on full-service lunches declined by 12 percent between 2006 and 2010, after adjusting for inflation. Behind the decline in spending was belt-tightening during the Great Recession. Spending on full-service lunches may increase in the years ahead as more boomers become empty-nesters with free time to enjoy a leisurely meal—but only if discretionary income grows.

Table 38. Lunch at full-service restaurants

Total household spending $34,533,661,050.00
Average household spends   285.15

	AVERAGE HOUSEHOLD SPENDING	BEST CUSTOMERS (index)	BIGGEST CUSTOMERS (market share)
AGE OF HOUSEHOLDER			
Average household	**$285.15**	**100**	**100.0%**
Under age 25	175.25	61	4.1
Aged 25 to 34	270.00	95	15.8
Aged 35 to 44	310.45	109	19.7
Aged 45 to 54	266.53	93	19.3
Aged 55 to 64	294.55	103	18.2
Aged 65 to 74	341.40	120	12.9
Aged 75 or older	301.38	106	10.1

	AVERAGE HOUSEHOLD SPENDING	BEST CUSTOMERS (index)	BIGGEST CUSTOMERS (market share)
HOUSEHOLD INCOME			
Average household	**$285.15**	**100**	**100.0%**
Under $20,000	128.68	45	9.8
$20,000 to $39,999	171.87	60	13.8
$40,000 to $49,999	238.32	84	7.9
$50,000 to $69,999	273.38	96	13.7
$70,000 to $79,999	429.54	151	9.0
$80,000 to $99,999	356.64	125	10.4
$100,000 or more	597.91	210	36.0
HOUSEHOLD TYPE			
Average household	**285.15**	**100**	**100.0**
Married couples	370.96	130	64.2
Married couples, no children	389.77	137	29.0
Married couples, with children	357.49	125	29.2
Oldest child under age 6	324.18	114	4.9
Oldest child aged 6 to 17	370.81	130	15.3
Oldest child aged 18 or older	354.67	124	9.0
Single parent with child under age 18	88.02	31	1.8
Single person	208.77	73	21.4
RACE AND HISPANIC ORIGIN			
Average household	**285.15**	**100**	**100.0**
Asian	394.72	138	5.9
Black	161.35	57	6.9
Hispanic	262.50	92	11.2
Non-Hispanic white and other	308.23	108	82.0
REGION			
Average household	**285.15**	**100**	**100.0**
Northeast	303.85	107	19.6
Midwest	205.27	72	16.0
South	305.71	107	39.3
West	316.77	111	25.2
EDUCATION			
Average household	**285.15**	**100**	**100.0**
Less than high school graduate	166.95	59	8.4
High school graduate	201.45	71	18.0
Some college	246.50	86	18.2
Associate's degree	283.67	99	9.4
Bachelor's degree or more	439.58	154	45.8
Bachelor's degree	421.24	148	27.9
Master's, professional, doctoral degree	475.69	167	18.0

Note: Market shares may not sum to 100.0 because of rounding and missing categories by household type. "Asian" and "black" include Hispanics and non-Hispanics who identify themselves as being of the respective race alone. "Hispanic" includes people of any race who identify themselves as Hispanic. "Other" includes people who identify themselves as non-Hispanic and as Alaska Native, American Indian, Asian (who are also included in the "Asian" row), Native Hawaiian or other Pacific Islander, as well as non-Hispanics reporting more than one race.
Source: Calculations by New Strategist based on the Bureau of Labor Statistics' 2010 Consumer Expenditure Survey

Restaurant and Carry-out Food on Trips

Best customers: Householders aged 45 to 74
Married couples without children at home
Married couples with school-aged or older children at home
Asians

Customer trends: Average household spending on restaurant and carry-out food on trips should grow as boomers retire, but only if discretionary income rises.

The biggest spenders on restaurant and carry-out meals on trips are the most-avid travelers—older married couples. Householders ranging in age from 45 to 74 spend 21 to 22 percent more than average on this item. Married couples without children at home (most of them empty-nesters) spend 63 percent more than average on restaurant and carry-out meals on trips and control over one-third of the market. Those with school-aged or older children at home spend 28 to 58 percent more. Asians, the most-affluent racial and ethnic group, spend 41 percent more than average on eating out while traveling.

Average household spending on restaurant and carry-out meals on trips fell 15 percent between 2006 and 2010, after adjusting for inflation. Behind the decline was household budget cutting in the midst of the Great Recession. Spending on this item should grow in the years ahead as boomers retire, but only if discretionary income grows.

Table 39. Restaurant and carry-out food on trips

Total household spending $27,016,549,560.00
Average household spends 223.08

	AVERAGE HOUSEHOLD SPENDING	BEST CUSTOMERS (index)	BIGGEST CUSTOMERS (market share)
AGE OF HOUSEHOLDER			
Average household	**$223.08**	**100**	**100.0%**
Under age 25	82.60	37	2.5
Aged 25 to 34	171.66	77	12.8
Aged 35 to 44	240.46	108	19.5
Aged 45 to 54	271.80	122	25.2
Aged 55 to 64	269.45	121	21.3
Aged 65 to 74	272.54	122	13.1
Aged 75 or older	130.35	58	5.6

	AVERAGE HOUSEHOLD SPENDING	BEST CUSTOMERS (index)	BIGGEST CUSTOMERS (market share)
HOUSEHOLD INCOME			
Average household	**$223.08**	**100**	**100.0%**
Under $20,000	49.53	22	4.8
$20,000 to $39,999	98.01	44	10.1
$40,000 to $49,999	139.46	63	5.9
$50,000 to $69,999	222.87	100	14.3
$70,000 to $79,999	255.80	115	6.9
$80,000 to $99,999	293.88	132	11.0
$100,000 or more	611.50	274	47.0
HOUSEHOLD TYPE			
Average household	**223.08**	**100**	**100.0**
Married couples	322.33	144	71.3
Married couples, no children	364.26	163	34.7
Married couples, with children	305.34	137	31.8
Oldest child under age 6	208.67	94	4.0
Oldest child aged 6 to 17	352.16	158	18.6
Oldest child aged 18 or older	286.42	128	9.3
Single parent with child under age 18	116.19	52	3.1
Single person	120.46	54	15.8
RACE AND HISPANIC ORIGIN			
Average household	**223.08**	**100**	**100.0**
Asian	315.10	141	6.0
Black	92.11	41	5.1
Hispanic	136.54	61	7.5
Non-Hispanic white and other	258.53	116	87.9
REGION			
Average household	**223.08**	**100**	**100.0**
Northeast	242.63	109	20.0
Midwest	224.79	101	22.5
South	186.37	84	30.7
West	265.03	119	26.9
EDUCATION			
Average household	**223.08**	**100**	**100.0**
Less than high school graduate	70.89	32	4.5
High school graduate	117.18	53	13.4
Some college	185.98	83	17.5
Associate's degree	216.19	97	9.2
Bachelor's degree or more	415.72	186	55.4
Bachelor's degree	377.29	169	31.9
Master's, professional, doctoral degree	482.81	216	23.4

Note: Market shares may not sum to 100.0 because of rounding and missing categories by household type. "Asian" and "black" include Hispanics and non-Hispanics who identify themselves as being of the respective race alone. "Hispanic" includes people of any race who identify themselves as Hispanic. "Other" includes people who identify themselves as non-Hispanic and as Alaska Native, American Indian, Asian (who are also included in the "Asian" row), Native Hawaiian or other Pacific Islander, as well as non-Hispanics reporting more than one race.
Source: Calculations by New Strategist based on the Bureau of Labor Statistics' 2010 Consumer Expenditure Survey

Snacks at Employer and School Cafeterias

Best customers: Householders under age 45
Married couples with children under age 18
Single parents
Asians
Households in the Northeast

Customer trends: Average household spending on snacks at employer and school cafeterias may continue its decline as fewer employers provide cafeterias in an attempt to cut costs.

Not surprisingly, parents and workers are the biggest spenders on snacks at employer and school cafeterias. Householders under age 35, most of them at school or in the workforce, spend 39 to 41 percent more than average on this item, and those aged 35 to 44 spend twice the average. Together these age groups account for 69 percent of the market. Married couples with preschoolers spend 40 percent more than average on cafeteria snacks, and those with school-aged children spend nearly three times the average on this item. Single parents, whose spending approaches average on only a few items, spend 9 percent more than average on this item. Asian householders spend well over two-and-one-half times the average on snacks at employer and school cafeterias. Households in the Northeast outspend the average by 30 percent.

Average household spending on snacks at employer and school cafeterias fell a substantial 20 percent between 2006 and 2010, after adjusting for inflation. In the years ahead, average household spending on snacks at employer and school cafeterias may continue its decline as employers cut costs by eliminating cafeterias.

Table 40. Snacks at employer and school cafeterias

Total household spending $718,164,510.00
Average household spends   5.93

AGE OF HOUSEHOLDER	AVERAGE HOUSEHOLD SPENDING	BEST CUSTOMERS (index)	BIGGEST CUSTOMERS (market share)
Average household	**$5.93**	**100**	**100.0%**
Under age 25	8.38	141	9.4
Aged 25 to 34	8.23	139	23.1
Aged 35 to 44	12.06	203	36.8
Aged 45 to 54	4.83	81	16.9
Aged 55 to 64	3.15	53	9.4
Aged 65 to 74	1.73	29	3.1
Aged 75 or older	1.06	18	1.7

	AVERAGE HOUSEHOLD SPENDING	BEST CUSTOMERS (index)	BIGGEST CUSTOMERS (market share)
HOUSEHOLD INCOME			
Average household	**$5.93**	**100**	**100.0%**
Under $20,000	3.01	51	11.1
$20,000 to $39,999	4.68	79	18.1
$40,000 to $49,999	4.89	82	7.8
$50,000 to $69,999	4.57	77	11.1
$70,000 to $79,999	15.70	265	15.8
$80,000 to $99,999	9.66	163	13.6
$100,000 or more	8.20	138	23.7
HOUSEHOLD TYPE			
Average household	**5.93**	**100**	**100.0**
Married couples	7.35	124	61.1
Married couples, no children	3.50	59	12.5
Married couples, with children	11.70	197	45.9
Oldest child under age 6	8.28	140	6.0
Oldest child aged 6 to 17	17.29	292	34.3
Oldest child aged 18 or older	5.11	86	6.2
Single parent with child under age 18	6.49	109	6.5
Single person	3.41	58	16.8
RACE AND HISPANIC ORIGIN			
Average household	**5.93**	**100**	**100.0**
Asian	16.23	274	11.6
Black	3.20	54	6.6
Hispanic	5.74	97	11.8
Non-Hispanic white and other	6.38	108	81.6
REGION			
Average household	**5.93**	**100**	**100.0**
Northeast	7.70	130	23.8
Midwest	4.37	74	16.4
South	6.12	103	37.9
West	5.75	97	22.0
EDUCATION			
Average household	**5.93**	**100**	**100.0**
Less than high school graduate	3.13	53	7.5
High school graduate	3.12	53	13.4
Some college	8.06	136	28.6
Associate's degree	3.46	58	5.5
Bachelor's degree or more	8.91	150	44.6
Bachelor's degree	8.26	139	26.3
Master's, professional, doctoral degree	10.18	172	18.6

Note: Market shares may not sum to 100.0 because of rounding and missing categories by household type. "Asian" and "black" include Hispanics and non-Hispanics who identify themselves as being of the respective race alone. "Hispanic" includes people of any race who identify themselves as Hispanic. "Other" includes people who identify themselves as non-Hispanic and as Alaska Native, American Indian, Asian (who are also included in the "Asian" row), Native Hawaiian or other Pacific Islander, as well as non-Hispanics reporting more than one race.
Source: Calculations by New Strategist based on the Bureau of Labor Statistics' 2010 Consumer Expenditure Survey

Snacks at Fast-Food Restaurants, Including Take-Outs, Deliveries, Concession Stands, Buffets, and Cafeterias (except Employer and School)

Best customers: Householders aged 25 to 44
Married couples with children at home
Asians
Households in the West

Customer trends: Average household spending on snacks at fast-food restaurants should stabilize or even increase in the years ahead as the large millennial generation moves into the best-customer lifestage.

Parents are the best customers of snacks from fast-food restaurants. Householders aged 25 to 44, most with children, spend 20 to 51 percent more than the average household on fast-food snacks. Married couples with children at home spend 67 percent more than average on this item, the figure peaking at 85 percent above average among parents with school-aged children. The spending on fast-food snacks by Asian householders is one-quarter higher than average. Households in the West outspend the average on fast-food snacks by 28 percent.

Average household spending on snacks from fast-food restaurants fell 12 percent between 2006 and 2010, after adjusting for inflation. Behind the decline was belt-tightening due to the Great Recession. Spending on this item should stabilize or even increase in the years ahead as the large millennial generation moves into the best-customer lifestage.

Table 41. Snacks at fast-food restaurants, including take-outs, deliveries, concession stands, buffets, and cafeterias (except employer and school)

Total household spending $12,383,190,750.00
Average household spends   102.25

	AVERAGE HOUSEHOLD SPENDING	BEST CUSTOMERS (index)	BIGGEST CUSTOMERS (market share)
AGE OF HOUSEHOLDER			
Average household	**$102.25**	**100**	**100.0%**
Under age 25	91.26	89	5.9
Aged 25 to 34	122.66	120	20.0
Aged 35 to 44	154.03	151	27.3
Aged 45 to 54	110.82	108	22.4
Aged 55 to 64	91.71	90	15.8
Aged 65 to 74	56.82	56	6.0
Aged 75 or older	29.06	28	2.7

	AVERAGE HOUSEHOLD SPENDING	BEST CUSTOMERS (index)	BIGGEST CUSTOMERS (market share)
HOUSEHOLD INCOME			
Average household	**$102.25**	**100**	**100.0%**
Under $20,000	44.56	44	9.5
$20,000 to $39,999	63.29	62	14.2
$40,000 to $49,999	83.63	82	7.7
$50,000 to $69,999	117.67	115	16.5
$70,000 to $79,999	135.44	132	7.9
$80,000 to $99,999	129.10	126	10.5
$100,000 or more	204.18	200	34.2
HOUSEHOLD TYPE			
Average household	**102.25**	**100**	**100.0**
Married couples	131.22	128	63.3
Married couples, no children	87.52	86	18.2
Married couples, with children	170.88	167	38.9
Oldest child under age 6	149.97	147	6.3
Oldest child aged 6 to 17	189.15	185	21.8
Oldest child aged 18 or older	154.34	151	10.9
Single parent with child under age 18	78.08	76	4.5
Single person	55.38	54	15.9
RACE AND HISPANIC ORIGIN			
Average household	**102.25**	**100**	**100.0**
Asian	127.59	125	5.3
Black	74.75	73	8.9
Hispanic	107.11	105	12.8
Non-Hispanic white and other	105.75	103	78.4
REGION			
Average household	**102.25**	**100**	**100.0**
Northeast	115.40	113	20.7
Midwest	90.86	89	19.8
South	85.56	84	30.7
West	130.47	128	28.9
EDUCATION			
Average household	**102.25**	**100**	**100.0**
Less than high school graduate	65.32	64	9.1
High school graduate	74.99	73	18.7
Some college	98.38	96	20.2
Associate's degree	125.60	123	11.6
Bachelor's degree or more	137.50	134	40.0
Bachelor's degree	139.89	137	25.8
Master's, professional, doctoral degree	132.80	130	14.1

Note: Market shares may not sum to 100.0 because of rounding and missing categories by household type. "Asian" and "black" include Hispanics and non-Hispanics who identify themselves as being of the respective race alone. "Hispanic" includes people of any race who identify themselves as Hispanic. "Other" includes people who identify themselves as non-Hispanic and as Alaska Native, American Indian, Asian (who are also included in the "Asian" row), Native Hawaiian or other Pacific Islander, as well as non-Hispanics reporting more than one race.
Source: Calculations by New Strategist based on the Bureau of Labor Statistics' 2010 Consumer Expenditure Survey

Snacks at Full-Service Restaurants

Best customers: Householders aged 25 to 34 and 45 to 64
Married couples with adult children at home
People who live alone
Households in the Northeast

Customer trends: Average household spending on snacks at full-service restaurants should rise in the years ahead as casual sit-down restaurants compete with fast-food establishments for the dollars of snackers.

The biggest spenders on snacks at full-service restaurants are young adults and middle-aged married couples with children. Householders aged 25 to 34 spend 19 percent more than average on snacks at full-service restaurants, and those aged 45 to 64 spend 11 to 17 percent more. Married couples with adult children at home spend 54 percent more than average on this item. People who live alone, whose spending is well below average on most items, spend 6 percent more than average on snacks at full-service restaurants. Households in the Northeast outspend the average on this item by 53 percent.

Average household spending on snacks at full-service restaurants fell by 11 percent between 2006 and 2010, after adjusting for inflation. Behind the decline was belt-tightening during the Great Recession. Spending on this item should grow in the years ahead as casual sit-down restaurants compete with fast-food establishments for the dollars of snackers.

Table 42. Snacks at full-service restaurants

Total household spending $3,455,182,710.00
Average household spends   28.53

	AVERAGE HOUSEHOLD SPENDING	BEST CUSTOMERS (index)	BIGGEST CUSTOMERS (market share)
AGE OF HOUSEHOLDER			
Average household	**$28.53**	**100**	**100.0%**
Under age 25	31.02	109	7.2
Aged 25 to 34	33.85	119	19.8
Aged 35 to 44	26.10	91	16.6
Aged 45 to 54	33.37	117	24.2
Aged 55 to 64	31.81	111	19.7
Aged 65 to 74	21.85	77	8.2
Aged 75 or older	12.52	44	4.2

	AVERAGE HOUSEHOLD SPENDING	BEST CUSTOMERS (index)	BIGGEST CUSTOMERS (market share)
HOUSEHOLD INCOME			
Average household	**$28.53**	**100**	**100.0%**
Under $20,000	10.86	38	8.3
$20,000 to $39,999	21.68	76	17.4
$40,000 to $49,999	18.45	65	6.1
$50,000 to $69,999	30.91	108	15.5
$70,000 to $79,999	37.42	131	7.9
$80,000 to $99,999	32.54	114	9.5
$100,000 or more	59.97	210	36.0
HOUSEHOLD TYPE			
Average household	**28.53**	**100**	**100.0**
Married couples	29.84	105	51.6
Married couples, no children	29.89	105	22.3
Married couples, with children	31.94	112	26.0
Oldest child under age 6	17.18	60	2.6
Oldest child aged 6 to 17	28.99	102	11.9
Oldest child aged 18 or older	43.89	154	11.1
Single parent with child under age 18	10.02	35	2.1
Single person	30.11	106	30.9
RACE AND HISPANIC ORIGIN			
Average household	**28.53**	**100**	**100.0**
Asian	25.86	91	3.9
Black	18.56	65	8.0
Hispanic	29.06	102	12.4
Non-Hispanic white and other	30.04	105	79.8
REGION			
Average household	**28.53**	**100**	**100.0**
Northeast	43.79	153	28.2
Midwest	25.19	88	19.7
South	20.37	71	26.2
West	32.83	115	26.1
EDUCATION			
Average household	**28.53**	**100**	**100.0**
Less than high school graduate	11.20	39	5.6
High school graduate	29.08	102	26.0
Some college	23.52	82	17.3
Associate's degree	22.42	79	7.4
Bachelor's degree or more	41.41	145	43.1
Bachelor's degree	39.68	139	26.3
Master's, professional, doctoral degree	44.81	157	17.0

Note: Market shares may not sum to 100.0 because of rounding and missing categories by household type. "Asian" and "black" include Hispanics and non-Hispanics who identify themselves as being of the respective race alone. "Hispanic" includes people of any race who identify themselves as Hispanic. "Other" includes people who identify themselves as non-Hispanic and as Alaska Native, American Indian, Asian (who are also included in the "Asian" row), Native Hawaiian or other Pacific Islander, as well as non-Hispanics reporting more than one race.
Source: Calculations by New Strategist based on the Bureau of Labor Statistics' 2010 Consumer Expenditure Survey

Snacks at Vending Machines and Mobile Vendors

Best customers:
Householders under age 55
Married couples with school-aged or older children at home
Single parents
Asians and Hispanics
Households in the Northeast

Customer trends:
Average household spending on snacks from vending machines and mobile vendors may continue to decline as restaurants and supermarkets compete for snack dollars.

The biggest spenders on snacks from vending machines and mobile vendors are the youngest householders and parents with children. Householders under age 25 spend 75 percent more than average on this item. Householders ranging in age from 25 to 54, most of them parents, spend 15 to 31 percent more than average on snacks from vending machines and mobile vendors. Married couples with school-aged or older children at home spend 26 to 55 percent more than average on vending machine snacks, and single parents, whose spending approaches average on only a few items, spend 45 percent more than average on this item. Asians spend 52 percent more than average on snacks from machines and street vendors, and Hispanics spend 26 percent more. Households in the Northeast outspend the average by 17 percent.

Average household spending on snacks from vending machines and mobile vendors fell by a steep 44 percent between 2006 and 2010, after adjusting for inflation. Spending on this category may continue to decline in the years ahead as fast-food and full-service restaurants, as well as grocery stores, compete for the snack dollar.

Table 43. Snacks at vending machines and mobile vendors

Total household spending $2,251,379,130.00
Average household spends   18.59

	AVERAGE HOUSEHOLD SPENDING	BEST CUSTOMERS (index)	BIGGEST CUSTOMERS (market share)
AGE OF HOUSEHOLDER			
Average household	**$18.59**	**100**	**100.0%**
Under age 25	32.53	175	11.6
Aged 25 to 34	21.38	115	19.2
Aged 35 to 44	24.35	131	23.7
Aged 45 to 54	23.34	126	26.0
Aged 55 to 64	14.94	80	14.2
Aged 65 to 74	6.71	36	3.9
Aged 75 or older	2.78	15	1.4

	AVERAGE HOUSEHOLD SPENDING	BEST CUSTOMERS (index)	BIGGEST CUSTOMERS (market share)
HOUSEHOLD INCOME			
Average household	**$18.59**	**100**	**100.0%**
Under $20,000	13.70	74	16.1
$20,000 to $39,999	17.54	94	21.6
$40,000 to $49,999	22.16	119	11.3
$50,000 to $69,999	17.79	96	13.7
$70,000 to $79,999	19.81	107	6.4
$80,000 to $99,999	20.29	109	9.1
$100,000 or more	24.16	130	22.3
HOUSEHOLD TYPE			
Average household	**18.59**	**100**	**100.0**
Married couples	20.27	109	53.8
Married couples, no children	13.11	71	15.0
Married couples, with children	25.24	136	31.6
Oldest child under age 6	18.34	99	4.2
Oldest child aged 6 to 17	28.83	155	18.2
Oldest child aged 18 or older	23.43	126	9.1
Single parent with child under age 18	26.92	145	8.5
Single person	12.14	65	19.1
RACE AND HISPANIC ORIGIN			
Average household	**18.59**	**100**	**100.0**
Asian	28.30	152	6.5
Black	13.31	72	8.8
Hispanic	23.46	126	15.4
Non-Hispanic white and other	18.65	100	76.1
REGION			
Average household	**18.59**	**100**	**100.0**
Northeast	21.77	117	21.5
Midwest	18.44	99	22.1
South	18.77	101	37.1
West	15.85	85	19.3
EDUCATION			
Average household	**18.59**	**100**	**100.0**
Less than high school graduate	16.19	87	12.4
High school graduate	20.50	110	28.2
Some college	21.73	117	24.6
Associate's degree	17.10	92	8.7
Bachelor's degree or more	16.20	87	25.9
Bachelor's degree	16.31	88	16.6
Master's, professional, doctoral degree	16.00	86	9.3

Note: Market shares may not sum to 100.0 because of rounding and missing categories by household type. "Asian" and "black" include Hispanics and non-Hispanics who identify themselves as being of the respective race alone. "Hispanic" includes people of any race who identify themselves as Hispanic. "Other" includes people who identify themselves as non-Hispanic and as Alaska Native, American Indian, Asian (who are also included in the "Asian" row), Native Hawaiian or other Pacific Islander, as well as non-Hispanics reporting more than one race.
Source: Calculations by New Strategist based on the Bureau of Labor Statistics' 2010 Consumer Expenditure Survey

Appendix
Spending by product and service ranked by amount spent, 2010

(average annual spending of consumer units on products and services, ranked by amount spent, 2010)

1.	Deductions for Social Security	$3,902.53
2.	Groceries (also shown by individual category)	3,624.04
3.	Mortgage interest (or rent, $2,773.24)	3,154.47
4.	Vehicle purchases (net outlay)	2,588.40
5.	Gasoline and motor oil	2,132.31
6.	Restaurants (also shown by meal category)	2,080.95
7.	Health insurance	1,830.53
8.	Property taxes	1,813.84
9.	Electricity	1,412.54
10.	Federal income taxes	1,135.67
11.	Vehicle insurance	1,010.42
12.	Dinner at restaurants	986.99
13.	Vehicle maintenance and repairs	787.28
14.	Cellular phone service	759.68
15.	Lunch at restaurants	726.61
16.	College tuition	701.62
17.	Cash contributions to church, religious organizations	661.03
18.	Cable and satellite television services	621.49
19.	Deductions for private pensions	588.76
20.	Maintenance and repair services, owner	576.13
21.	Women's apparel	561.50
22.	State and local income taxes	482.45
23.	Nonpayroll deposit to retirement plans	469.09
24.	Natural gas	439.97
25.	Alcoholic beverages	411.97
26.	Residential telephone service and pay phones	401.31
27.	Cash gifts to members of other households	398.06
28.	Water and sewerage maintenance	360.40
29.	Prescription drugs	350.07
30.	Homeowner's insurance	344.52
31.	Cigarettes	331.80
32.	Airline fares	325.31
33.	Life and other personal insurance	318.12
34.	Men's apparel	304.05
35.	Lodging on trips	299.03
36.	Computer information services	285.14
37.	Owned vacation homes	278.94
38.	Personal care services	277.26
39.	Dental services	262.62
40.	Vehicle finance charges	243.03
41.	Day care centers, nurseries, and preschools	238.57
42.	Fresh fruits	232.24
43.	Restaurant meals on trips	223.08
44.	Child support expenditures	220.09
45.	Beef	216.70
46.	Breakfast at restaurants	212.05
47.	Fresh vegetables	210.47
48.	Interest paid, home equity loan/line of credit	196.74
49.	Finance charges, except mortgage and vehicles	185.98
50.	Physician's services	183.17
51.	Pet food	165.20
52.	Leased vehicles	164.11
53.	Pet purchase, supplies, and medicines	162.51
54.	Cash contributions to charities	159.51

55.	Elementary and high school tuition	$156.02
56.	Snacks at restaurants	155.29
57.	Movie, theater, amusement park, and other admissions	155.00
58.	Other taxes	151.07
59.	Laundry and cleaning supplies	150.26
60.	Pork	148.99
61.	Prepared foods except frozen, salads, and desserts	146.76
62.	Women's footwear	146.30
63.	Computers and computer hardware for nonbusiness use	144.58
64.	Poultry	138.12
65.	Cosmetics, perfume, and bath products	134.20
66.	Carbonated drinks	132.65
67.	Miscellaneous household products	129.52
68.	Legal fees	128.73
69.	Trash and garbage collection	125.49
70.	Fresh milk, all types	121.03
71.	Social, recreational, health club membership	120.72
72.	Television sets	118.73
73.	Toys, games, hobbies, and tricycles	117.78
74.	Fish and seafood	117.08
75.	Hospital room and services	115.48
76.	Cheese	115.43
77.	Veterinarian services	113.52
78.	Housekeeping services	111.70
79.	Vehicle registration	110.90
80.	Fees for participant sports	108.25
81.	Gardening, lawn care service	107.66
82.	Expenses for other properties	107.28
83.	Cleansing and toilet tissue, paper towels, and napkins	103.41
84.	Beer and ale at home	102.83
85.	Household decorative items	101.37
86.	Men's footwear	101.14
87.	Girls' (aged 2 to 15) apparel	101.10
88.	Potato chips and other snacks	99.32
89.	Support for college students	97.78
90.	Jewelry	96.48
91.	Lawn and garden supplies	96.09
92.	Fees for recreational lessons	94.41
93.	Miscellaneous personal services	92.06
94.	Children's (under age 2) apparel	90.58
95.	Deductions for government retirement	90.40
96.	Nonprescription drugs	89.56
97.	Wine at home	87.69
98.	Sofas	84.27
99.	Ready-to-eat and cooked cereals	82.83
100.	Lunch meats (cold cuts)	81.80
101.	Rent as pay	80.63
102.	Babysitting and child care	79.51
103.	Funeral expenses	79.36
104.	Lottery and gambling losses	78.72
105.	Boys' (aged 2 to 15) apparel	77.77
106.	Fuel oil	77.47
107.	Candy and chewing gum	77.34
108.	Stationery, stationery supplies, giftwrap	73.27
109.	Frozen prepared foods, except meals	71.17
110.	Catered affairs	70.71
111.	Maintenance and repair materials, owner	68.48
112.	Intracity mass transit fares	66.87
113.	Motorized recreational vehicles	66.42
114.	Unmotored recreational vehicles	65.77
115.	Accounting fees	65.52
116.	Books and supplies for college	63.79

117.	School lunches	$63.40
118.	Beer and ale at bars, restaurants	62.96
119.	Bedroom furniture except mattresses and springs	62.56
120.	Hair care products	62.00
121.	Frozen meals	60.95
122.	Eyeglasses and contact lenses	60.64
123.	Coffee	60.25
124.	Bread, other than white	59.72
125.	Admission to sports events	59.62
126.	Refrigerators and freezers	58.14
127.	Ground rent	58.00
128.	Housing while attending school	57.11
129.	Postage	56.06
130.	Ice cream and related products	54.26
131.	Service by professionals other than physician	54.00
132.	Bottled gas	53.88
133.	Property management, owner	53.59
134.	Watches	53.09
135.	Canned vegetables	52.51
136.	Sauces and gravies	52.44
137.	Bottled water	52.04
138.	Canned and bottled fruit juice	51.97
139.	Occupational expenses	51.64
140.	Other alcoholic beverages at bars, restaurants	51.31
141.	Video game hardware and software	50.80
142.	Professional laundry, dry cleaning	49.53
143.	Biscuits and rolls	48.84
144.	Mattresses and springs	48.62
145.	Athletic gear, game tables, exercise equipment	47.28
146.	Other dairy (yogurt, etc.)	46.80
147.	Eggs	46.29
148.	Books	46.09
149.	Bedroom linens	45.95
150.	Cookies	45.90
151.	Nonprescription vitamins	45.54
152.	Moving, storage, and freight express	44.74
153.	Lab tests, X-rays	44.69
154.	Food prepared by consumer unit on trips	43.36
155.	Alcoholic beverages purchased on trips	42.71
156.	Indoor plants and fresh flowers	42.60
157.	Canned and packaged soups	42.30
158.	Wall units, cabinets, and other furniture	40.97
159.	Newspaper and magazine subscriptions	39.90
160.	White bread	39.83
161.	Ship fares	39.34
162.	Power tools	39.23
163.	Coin-operated apparel laundry and dry cleaning	39.07
164.	Board (including at school)	38.94
165.	Pet services	38.87
166.	Parking fees	38.19
167.	Alimony expenditures	37.52
168.	Lawn and garden equipment	37.06
169.	Rented vehicles	36.78
170.	Living room chairs	36.47
171.	Crackers	36.26
172.	Topicals and dressings	36.17
173.	Frozen vegetables	36.16
174.	Cash contributions to educational institutions	35.86
175.	Prepared salads	35.43
176.	Cakes and cupcakes	35.30
177.	Deodorants, feminine hygiene, miscellaneous products	35.24
178.	Outdoor equipment	34.74

179. Eye care services	$34.65
180. Washing machines	34.04
181. Oral hygiene products	33.98
182. Pasta, cornmeal, and other cereal products	33.92
183. Nuts	33.65
184. Wine at bars, restaurants	33.30
185. Telephones and accessories	32.60
186. Salt, spices, and other seasonings	32.49
187. Baby food	32.48
188. Kitchen and dining room furniture	31.79
189. Fats and oils	31.49
190. Tea	29.20
191. Cooking stoves, ovens	28.81
192. Salad dressings	28.77
193. Tolls	28.72
194. Girls' footwear	28.62
195. Clothes dryers	27.92
196. Sound components, equipment, and accessories	27.67
197. Meals as pay	27.45
198. Video cassettes, tapes, and discs	27.38
199. Boys' footwear	27.32
200. Tobacco products other than cigarettes	26.52
201. Jams, preserves, other sweets	26.49
202. Outdoor furniture	26.39
203. Baking needs	26.18
204. Hunting and fishing equipment	26.17
205. Maintenance and repair services, renter	25.25
206. Frozen and refrigerated bakery products	25.19
207. Rice	24.72
208. Frankfurters	24.51
209. Noncarbonated fruit-flavored drinks	24.25
210. Photographic equipment	24.25
211. Home security system service fee	23.62
212. Tableware, nonelectric kitchenware	23.57
213. Butter	23.03
214. Window coverings	22.96
215. Sugar	22.76
216. Checking accounts, other bank service charges	22.44
217. Sweetrolls, coffee cakes, doughnuts	22.28
218. Lamps and lighting fixtures	21.93
219. Small electric kitchen appliances	21.85
220. Recreation expenses on trips	21.58
221. Rental of video cassettes, tapes, discs, films	21.51
222. Termite and pest control products and services	20.97
223. Care for elderly, invalids, handicapped, etc.	20.80
224. Canned fruits	20.53
225. Cream	19.88
226. School tuition other than college, vocational/technical, elementary, high school	19.55
227. Fresh fruit juice	19.16
228. Sports drinks	19.11
229. Appliance repair, including at service center	19.02
230. Other alcoholic beverages at home	18.98
231. Portable heating and cooling equipment	18.73
232. Wall-to-wall carpeting	18.69
233. Bathroom linens	18.68
234. Automobile service clubs	18.63
235. Dried vegetables	18.25
236. Shaving products	17.95
237. Laundry and cleaning equipment	17.83
238. Curtains and draperies	17.69
239. Dishwashers (built-in), garbage disposals, range hoods	17.45

240.	Floor coverings, nonpermanent	$17.38
241.	Nondairy cream and imitation milk	16.96
242.	Computer software and accessories for nonbusiness use	16.89
243.	Local transportation on trips	16.86
244.	Photographer fees	16.62
245.	Prepared desserts	16.53
246.	Infants' equipment	16.48
247.	Taxi fares and limousine service	16.43
248.	Pies, tarts, turnovers	16.30
249.	Living room tables	16.16
250.	Nonelectric cookware	16.07
251.	Closet and storage items	15.85
252.	Intercity train fares	15.67
253.	Electric floor-cleaning equipment	15.47
254.	Peanut butter	15.46
255.	Bicycles	15.43
256.	Musical instruments and accessories	15.26
257.	Prepared flour mixes	15.25
258.	Vegetable juices	15.14
259.	Nonalcoholic beverages (except carbonated, coffee, fruit-flavored drinks, and tea) and ice	15.12
260.	Cemetery lots, vaults, and maintenance fees	15.12
261.	Olives, pickles, relishes	14.86
262.	Satellite radio service	14.57
263.	Compact discs, records, and audio tapes	13.79
264.	Hand tools	13.76
265.	Camping equipment	13.41
266.	Books and supplies for elementary and high school	13.14
267.	Cash contributions to political organizations	12.80
268.	Rental of party supplies for catered affairs	12.73
269.	Luggage	12.64
270.	Newspapers and magazines, nonsubscription	12.63
271.	Hearing aids	12.38
272.	Tenant's insurance	12.28
273.	Whiskey at home	12.19
274.	Personal digital audio players	11.42
275.	Photo processing	11.42
276.	Vehicle inspection	11.37
277.	Electric personal care appliances	11.13
278.	Lamb, organ meats, and others	10.88
279.	Gifts of stocks, bonds, and mutual funds to members of other households	10.59
280.	Docking and landing fees	10.57
281.	Microwave ovens	10.54
282.	Intercity bus fares	10.34
283.	Live entertainment for catered affairs	10.34
284.	Test preparation, tutoring services	10.20
285.	VCRs and video disc players	10.10
286.	Glassware	10.01
287.	Margarine	9.92
288.	Sewing materials for household items	9.53
289.	Vocational and technical school tuition	9.19
290.	Driver's license	9.00
291.	Coal, wood, and other fuels	8.96
292.	Security services, owner	8.77
293.	Voice over IP	8.62
294.	Shopping club membership fees	8.50
295.	Dried fruits	8.20
296.	Phone cards	8.14
297.	Maintenance and repair materials, renter	8.11
298.	Infants' furniture	8.07
299.	Flour	7.89
300.	China and other dinnerware	7.52

301.	Bread and cracker products	$7.48
302.	Repair of computer systems for nonbusiness use	7.29
303.	Care in convalescent or nursing home	7.14
304.	Rental of recreational vehicles	7.13
305.	Hair accessories	7.11
306.	Repairs and rentals of lawn and garden equipment, hand and power tools, etc.	7.08
307.	Portable memory	7.06
308.	Frozen fruits	6.78
309.	Streamed and downloaded audio	6.70
310.	Reupholstering and furniture repair	6.21
311.	Apparel alteration, repair, and tailoring services	6.20
312.	Frozen fruit juices	6.11
313.	Office furniture for home use	6.06
314.	Kitchen and dining room linens	5.92
315.	Sewing patterns and notions	5.69
316.	Winter sports equipment	5.63
317.	Artificial sweeteners	5.40
318.	Global positioning system devices	5.20
319.	Window air conditioners	5.12
320.	Playground equipment	4.91
321.	Personal digital assistants	4.68
322.	Material for making clothes	4.46
323.	Water sports equipment	4.42
324.	Rental of furniture	4.18
325.	Flatware	4.13
326.	Towing charges	3.99
327.	Supportive and convalescent medical equipment	3.93
328.	Business equipment for home use	3.79
329.	Smoking accessories	3.74
330.	Slipcovers and decorative pillows	3.71
331.	Safe deposit box rental	3.65
332.	Deductions for railroad retirement	3.62
333.	Nonclothing laundry and dry cleaning, coin-operated	3.59
334.	Water-softening service	3.54
335.	Miscellaneous video equipment	3.51
336.	Vacation clubs	3.41
337.	Septic tank cleaning	3.40
338.	Watch and jewelry repair	3.22
339.	Wigs and hairpieces	3.19
340.	Delivery services	2.97
341.	Rental and repair of miscellaneous sports equipment	2.90
342.	Sewing machines	2.82
343.	Stamp and coin collecting	2.77
344.	Repair of TV, radio, and sound equipment	2.69
345.	Medical equipment for general use	2.67
346.	Parking at owned home	2.64
347.	Online gaming services	2.55
348.	Plastic dinnerware	2.41
349.	Rental of medical equipment	2.03
350.	Streamed and downloaded video	1.94
351.	Internet services away from home	1.86
352.	Pinball, electronic video games	1.78
353.	School bus	1.77
354.	Clothing rental	1.76
355.	Credit card memberships	1.72
356.	Global positioning services	1.62
357.	Shoe repair and other shoe services	1.54
358.	Smoke alarms	1.47
359.	Rental and repair of musical instruments	1.42
360.	Fireworks	1.31
361.	Other serving pieces	1.23

362.	Film	$1.23
363.	Satellite dishes	1.22
364.	Appliance rental	1.18
365.	Rental of supportive and convalescent medical equipment	1.18
366.	Nonclothing laundry and dry cleaning, sent out	1.06
367.	Books and supplies for vocational and technical schools	0.98
368.	Books and supplies for day care and nursery	0.49
369.	Rental of television sets	0.43
370.	Portable dishwashers	0.37
371.	Clothing storage	0.37
372.	Installation of television sets	0.37
373.	Rental of office equipment for nonbusiness use	0.36
374.	Repair and rental of photographic equipment	0.35
375.	Telephone answering devices	0.34
376.	Dating services	0.32
377.	Installation of computer	0.31
378.	Rental of computer and video game hardware and software	0.15
379.	Rental of VCR, radio, and sound equipment	0.04

Source: Calculations by New Strategist based on the 2010 Consumer Expenditure Survey

Glossary

age. The age of the reference person.

alcoholic beverages. Includes beer and ale, wine, whiskey, gin, vodka, rum, and other alcoholic beverages.

annual spending. The annual amount spent per household. The Bureau of Labor Statistics calculates the annual average for all households in a segment, not just for those that purchased an item. The averages are calculated by integrating the results of the diary (weekly) and interview (quarterly) portions of the Consumer Expenditure Survey. For items purchased by most households—such as bread—average annual spending figures are a fairly accurate account of actual spending. For products and services purchased by few households during a year's time—such as cars—the average annual amount spent is much less than what purchasers spend.

apparel, accessories, and related services. Includes the following:
• *men's and boys' apparel.* Includes coats, jackets, sweaters, vests, sport coats, tailored jackets, slacks, shorts and short sets, sportswear, shirts, underwear, nightwear, hosiery, uniforms, and other accessories.
• *women's and girls' apparel.* Includes coats, jackets, furs, sport coats, tailored jackets, sweaters, vests, blouses, shirts, dresses, dungarees, culottes, slacks, shorts, sportswear, underwear, nightwear, uniforms, hosiery, and other accessories.
• *infants' apparel.* Includes coats, jackets, snowsuits, underwear, diapers, dresses, crawlers, sleeping garments, hosiery, footwear, and other accessories for children.
• *footwear.* Includes articles such as shoes, slippers, boots, and other similar items. It excludes footwear for babies and footwear used for sports such as bowling or golf shoes.
• *other apparel products and services.* Includes material for making clothes, shoe repair, alterations and sewing patterns and notions, clothing rental, clothing storage, dry cleaning, sent-out laundry, watches, jewelry, and repairs to watches and jewelry.

baby boom. Americans born between 1946 and 1964.

cash contributions. Includes cash contributed to persons or organizations outside the consumer unit including court-ordered alimony, child support payments, support for college students, and contributions to religious, educational, charitable, or political organizations.

consumer unit (1) All members of a household who are related by blood, marriage, adoption, or other legal arrangements; (2) a person living alone or sharing a household with others or living as a roomer in a private home or lodging house or in permanent living quarters in a hotel or motel, but who is financially independent; or (3) two or more persons living together who pool their income to make joint expenditure decisions. Financial independence is determined by the three major expense categories: housing, food, and other living expenses. To be considered financially independent, at least two of the three major expense categories have to be provided by the respondent. For convenience, called household in the text of this report.

consumer unit, composition of. The classification of interview households by type according to (1) relationship of other household members to the reference person; (2) age of the children of the reference person; and (3) combination of relationship to the reference person and age of the children. Stepchildren and adopted children are included with the reference person's own children.

earner. A consumer unit member aged 14 or older who worked at least one week during the 12 months prior to the interview date.

education. Includes tuition, fees, books, supplies, and equipment for public and private nursery schools, elementary and high schools, colleges and universities, and other schools.

entertainment. Includes the following:
• *fees and admissions.* Includes fees for participant sports; admissions to sporting events, movies, concerts, plays; health, swimming, tennis, and country club memberships, and other social recreational and fraternal organizations; recreational lessons or instructions; and recreational expenses on trips.
• *audio and visual equipment and services.* Includes television sets; radios; cable TV; tape recorders and players; video cassettes, tapes, and discs; video cassette recorders and video disc players; video game hardware and software; personal digital audio players; streaming and downloading audio and video; sound components; CDs, records, and tapes; musical instruments; and rental and repair of TV and sound equipment.
• *pets, toys, hobbies, and playground equipment.* Includes pet food, pet services, veterinary expenses, toys, games, hobbies, and playground equipment.
• *other entertainment equipment and services.* Includes indoor exercise equipment, athletic shoes, bicycles, trailers, campers, camping equipment, rental of campers and trailers, hunting and fishing equipment, sports equipment, winter sports equipment, water sports equipment, boats, boat motors and boat trailers, rental of boats, landing and docking fees, rental and repair of sports equipment, photographic equipment, film, photo processing, photographer fees, repair and rental of photo equipment, fireworks, pinball and electronic video games.

expenditure. The transaction cost including excise and sales taxes of goods and services acquired during the survey period. The full cost of each purchase is recorded even though full payment may not have been made at the date of purchase. Expenditure estimates include gifts. Excluded from expenditures are purchases or portions of purchases directly assignable to business purposes and periodic credit or installment payments on goods and services already acquired.

federal income tax. Includes federal income tax withheld in the survey year to pay for income earned in survey year plus additional tax paid in survey year to cover any underpayment or underwithholding of tax in the year prior to the survey.

financial products and services. Includes accounting fees, legal fees, union dues, professional dues and fees, other occupational expenses, funerals, cemetery lots, dating services, shopping club memberships, and unclassified fees and personal services.

food. Includes the following:
• *food at home.* Refers to the total expenditures for food at grocery stores or other food stores during the interview period. It is calculated by multiplying the number of visits to a grocery or other food store by the average amount spent per visit. It excludes the purchase of nonfood items.
• *food away from home.* Includes all meals (breakfast, lunch, brunch, and dinner) at restaurants, carry-outs, and vending machines, including tips, plus meals as pay, special catered affairs such as weddings, bar mitzvahs, and confirmations, and meals away from home on trips.

generation X. Americans born between 1965 and 1976; also known as the baby-bust generation.

gifts for people in other households. Includes gift expenditures for people living in other consumer units. The amount spent on gifts is also included in individual product and service categories.

health care. Includes the following:

• *health insurance.* Includes health maintenance plans (HMOs), Blue Cross/Blue Shield, commercial health insurance, Medicare, Medicare supplemental insurance, long-term care insurance, and other health insurance.

• *medical services.* Includes hospital room and services, physicians' services, services of a practitioner other than a physician, eye and dental care, lab tests, X-rays, nursing, therapy services, care in convalescent or nursing home, and other medical care.

• *drugs.* Includes prescription and nonprescription drugs, internal and respiratory over-the-counter drugs.

• *medical supplies.* Includes eyeglasses and contact lenses, topicals and dressings, antiseptics, bandages, cotton, first aid kits, contraceptives; medical equipment for general use such as syringes, ice bags, thermometers, vaporizers, heating pads; supportive or convalescent medical equipment such as hearing aids, braces, canes, crutches, and walkers.

Hispanic origin. The self-identified Hispanic origin of the consumer unit reference person. All consumer units are included in one of two Hispanic origin groups based on the reference person's Hispanic origin: Hispanic or non-Hispanic. Hispanics may be of any race.

household. According to the Census Bureau, all the people who occupy a household. A group of unrelated people who share a housing unit as roommates or unmarried partners is also counted as a household. Households do not include group quarters such as college dormitories, prisons, or nursing homes. A household may contain more than one consumer unit. The terms "household" and "consumer unit" are used interchangeably in this report.

household furnishings and equipment. Includes the following:

• *household textiles.* Includes bathroom, kitchen, dining room, and other linens, curtains and drapes, slipcovers and decorative pillows, and sewing materials.

• *furniture.* Includes living room, dining room, kitchen, bedroom, nursery, porch, lawn, and other outdoor furniture.

• *carpet, rugs, and other floor coverings.* Includes installation and replacement of wall-to-wall carpets, room-size rugs, and other soft floor coverings.

• *major appliances.* Includes refrigerators, freezers, dishwashers, stoves, ovens, garbage disposals, vacuum cleaners, microwave ovens, air-conditioners, sewing machines, washing machines, clothes dryers, and floor-cleaning equipment.

• *small appliances and miscellaneous housewares.* Includes small electrical kitchen appliances, portable heating and cooling equipment, china and other dinnerware, flatware, glassware, silver and other serving pieces, nonelectric cookware, and plastic dinnerware. Excludes personal care appliances.

• *miscellaneous household equipment.* Includes computer hardware and software, luggage, lamps and other lighting fixtures, window coverings, clocks, lawn mowers and gardening equipment, hand and power tools, telephone answering devices, personal digital assistants, Internet services away from home, office equipment for home use, fresh flowers and house plants, rental of furniture, closet and storage items, household decorative items, infants' equipment, outdoor equipment, smoke alarms, other household appliances, and small miscellaneous furnishing.

household services. Includes the following:

• *personal services.* Includes baby sitting, day care, and care of elderly and handicapped persons.

• *other household services.* Includes computer information services; housekeeping services; gardening and lawn care services; coin-operated laundry and dry-cleaning of household textiles; termite and pest control products; moving, storage, and freight expenses; repair of household appliances and other household equipment; reupholstering and furniture repair; rental and repair of lawn and gardening tools; and rental of other household equipment.

housekeeping supplies. Includes soaps, detergents, other laundry cleaning products, cleansing and toilet tissue, paper towels, napkins, and miscellaneous household products; lawn and garden supplies, postage, stationery, stationery supplies, and gift wrap.

housing tenure. "Owner" includes households living in their own homes, cooperatives, condominiums, or townhouses. "Renter" includes households paying rent as well as families living rent free in lieu of wages.

income before taxes. The total money earnings and selected money receipts accruing to a consumer unit during the 12 months prior to the interview date. Income includes the following components:

• *wages and salaries.* Includes total money earnings for all members of the consumer unit aged 14 or older from all jobs, including civilian wages and salaries, Armed Forces pay and allowances, piece-rate payments, commissions, tips, National Guard or Reserve pay (received for training periods), and cash bonuses before deductions for taxes, pensions, union dues, etc.

• *self-employment income.* Includes net business and farm income, which consists of net income (gross receipts minus operating expenses) from a profession or unincorporated business or from the operation of a farm by an owner, tenant, or sharecropper. If the business or farm is a partnership, only an appropriate share of net income is recorded. Losses are also recorded.

• *Social Security, private and government retirement.* Includes payments by the federal government made under retirement, survivor, and disability insurance programs to retired persons, dependents of deceased insured workers, or to disabled workers; and private pensions or retirement benefits received by retired persons or their survivors, either directly or through an insurance company.

• *interest, dividends, rental income, and other property income* Includes interest income on savings or bonds; payments made by a corporation to its stockholders, periodic receipts from estates or trust funds; net income or loss from the rental of property, real estate, or farms, and net income or loss from roomers or boarders.

• *unemployment and workers' compensation and veterans' benefits.* Includes income from unemployment compensation and workers' compensation, and veterans' payments including educational benefits, but excluding military retirement.

• *public assistance, supplemental security income, and food stamps.* Includes public assistance or welfare, including money received from job training grants; supplemental security income paid by federal, state, and local welfare agencies to low-income persons who are aged 65 or older, blind, or disabled; and the value of food stamps obtained.

• *regular contributions for support.* Includes alimony and child support as well as any regular contributions from persons outside the consumer unit.

• *other income.* Includes money income from care of foster children, cash scholarships, fellowships, or stipends not based on working; and meals and rent as pay.

indexed spending. Indexed spending figures compare the spending of particular demographic segments with that of the average household. To compute an index, the amount spent on an item by a demographic segment is divided by the amount spent on the item by the average household. That figure is then multiplied by 100. An index of 100 is the average for all households. An index of 132 means average spending by households in a segment is 32 percent above average (100 plus 32). An index of 75 means average spending by households in a segment is 25 percent below average (100 minus 25). Indexed spending figures identify the consumer units that spend the most on a product or service.

life and other personal insurance. Includes premiums from whole life and term insurance; endowments; income and other life insurance; mortgage guarantee insurance; mortgage life insurance; premiums for personal life liability, accident and disability; and other non–health insurance other than homes and vehicles.

market share. The market share is the percentage of total household spending on an item that is accounted for by a demographic segment. Market shares are calculated by dividing a demographic segment's total spending on an item by the total spending of all households on the item. Total spending on an item for all households is calculated by multiplying average spending by the total number of households. Total spending on an item for each demographic segment is calculated by multiplying the segment's average spending by the number of households in the segment. Market shares reveal the demographic segments that account for the largest share of spending on a product or service.

millennial generation. Americans born between 1977 and 1994.

occupation. The occupation in which the reference person received the most earnings during the survey period. The occupational categories follow those of the Census of Population. Categories shown in the tables include the following:

• *self-employed.* Includes all occupational categories; the reference person is self-employed in own business, professional practice, or farm.

• *wage and salary earners, managers and professionals.* Includes executives, administrators, managers, and professional specialties such as architects, engineers, natural and social scientists, lawyers, teachers, writers, health diagnosis and treatment workers, entertainers, and athletes.

• *wage and salary earners, technical, sales, and clerical workers.* Includes technicians and related support workers; sales representatives, sales workers, cashiers, and sales-related occupations; and administrative support, including clerical.

• *retired.* People who did not work either full- or part-time during the survey period.

owner. *See* housing tenure.

pensions and Social Security. Includes all Social Security contributions paid by employees; employees' contributions to railroad retirement, government retirement and private pensions programs; retirement programs for self-employed.

personal care. Includes products for the hair, oral hygiene products, shaving needs, cosmetics, bath products, suntan lotions, hand creams, electric personal care appliances, incontinence products, other personal care products, personal care services such as hair care services (haircuts, bleaching, tinting, coloring, conditioning treatments, permanents, press, and curls), styling and other services for wigs and hairpieces, body massages or slenderizing treatments, facials, manicures, pedicures, shaves, electrolysis.

quarterly spending. Quarterly spending data are collected in the interview portion of the Consumer Expenditure Survey. The quarterly spending tables show the percentage of households that purchased an item during an average quarter, and the amount spent during the quarter on the item by purchasers. Not all items are included in the interview portion of the Consumer Expenditure Survey.

reading. Includes subscriptions for newspapers, magazines, and books through book clubs; purchase of single-copy newspapers and magazines, books, and encyclopedias and other reference books.

reference person. The first member mentioned by the respondent when asked to "Start with the name of the person or one of the persons who owns or rents the home." It is with respect to this person that the relationship of other consumer unit members is determined. Also called the householder or head of household.

region. Consumer units are classified according to their address at the time of their participation in the survey. The four major census regions of the United States are the following state groupings:

• *Northeast.* Connecticut, Maine, Massachusetts, New Hampshire, New Jersey, New York, Pennsylvania, Rhode Island, and Vermont.

• *Midwest.* Illinois, Indiana, Iowa, Kansas, Michigan, Minnesota, Mississippi, Nebraska, North Dakota, Ohio, South Dakota, and Wisconsin.

• *South.* Alabama, Arkansas, Delaware, District of Columbia, Florida, Georgia, Kentucky, Louisiana, Maryland, Mississippi, North Carolina, Oklahoma, South Carolina, Tennessee, Texas, Virginia, and West Virginia.

• *West.* Alaska, Arizona, California, Colorado, Hawaii, Idaho, Minnesota, Nevada, New Mexico, Oregon, Utah, Washington, and Wyoming.

renter. *See* housing tenure.

shelter. Includes the following:

• *owned dwellings.* Includes interest on mortgages, property taxes and insurance, refinancing and prepayment charges, ground rent, expenses for property management and security, homeowner's insurance, fire insurance and extended coverage, landscaping expenses for repairs and maintenance contracted out (including periodic maintenance and service contracts), and expenses of materials for owner-performed repairs and maintenance for dwellings used or maintained by the consumer unit, but not dwellings maintained for business or rent.

• *rented dwellings.* Includes rent paid for dwellings, rent received as pay, parking fees, maintenance, and other expenses.

• *other lodging.* Includes all expenses for vacation homes, school, college, hotels, motels, cottages, trailer camps, and other lodging while out of town.

• *utilities, fuels, and public services.* Includes natural gas, electricity, fuel oil, coal, bottled gas, wood, other fuels; residential telephone service, cell phone service, phone cards; water, garbage, trash collection; sewerage maintenance, septic tank cleaning; and other public services.

size of consumer unit. The number of people whose usual place of residence at the time of the interview is in the consumer unit.

state and local income taxes. Includes state and local income taxes withheld in the survey year to pay for income earned in survey year plus additional taxes paid in the survey year to cover any underpayment or underwithholding of taxes in the year prior to the survey.

tobacco and smoking supplies. Includes cigarettes, cigars, snuff, loose smoking tobacco, chewing tobacco, and smoking accessories such as cigarette or cigar holders, pipes, flints, lighters, pipe cleaners, and other smoking products and accessories.

transportation. Includes the following:

• *vehicle purchases (net outlay)*. Includes the net outlay (purchase price minus trade-in value) on new and used domestic and imported cars and trucks and other vehicles, including motorcycles and private planes.

• *gasoline and motor oil*. Includes gasoline, diesel fuel, and motor oil.

• *other vehicle expenses*. Includes vehicle finance charges, maintenance and repairs, vehicle insurance, and vehicle rental licenses and other charges.

• *vehicle finance charges*. Includes the dollar amount of interest paid for a loan contracted for the purchase of vehicles described above.

• *maintenance and repairs*. Includes tires, batteries, tubes, lubrication, filters, coolant, additives, brake and transmission fluids, oil change, brake adjustment and repair, front-end alignment, wheel balancing, steering repair, shock absorber replacement, clutch and transmission repair, electrical system repair, repair to cooling system, drive train repair, drive shaft and rear-end repair, tire repair, vehicle video equipment, other maintenance and services, and auto repair policies.

• *vehicle insurance*. Includes the premium paid for insuring cars, trucks, and other vehicles.

• *vehicle rental, licenses, and other charges*. Includes leased and rented cars, trucks, motorcycles, and aircraft, inspection fees, state and local registration, drivers' license fees, parking fees, towing charges, tolls on trips, and global positioning services.

• *public transportation*. Includes fares for mass transit, buses, trains, airlines, taxis, private school buses, and fares paid on trips for trains, boats, taxis, buses, and trains.

weekly spending Weekly spending data are collected in the diary portion of the Consumer Expenditure Survey. The data show the percentage of households that purchased an item during the average week, and the amount spent per week on the item by purchasers. Not all items are included in the diary portion of the Consumer Expenditure Survey.